CONTENTS

Reading & Writing in the Middle Years

DAVID BOOTH

Stenhouse Publishers
PORTLAND, MAINE

Pembroke Publishers Limited
MARKHAM, ONTARIO

For the kids on my porch over the years:
Michael, Leanne and Chris
Kim and Philip
Lisa and Laura
Steve and Bernard
and of course, as always, Jay

©2001   Pembroke Publishers
538 Hood Road
Markham, Ontario, Canada L3R 3K9
www.pembrokepublishers.com

Published in the United States by Stenhouse Publishers
477 Congress Street, Suite 4B
Portland, ME 04101
ISBN 1-57110-344-9
www.stenhouse.com

We acknowledge the financial support of the Government of Canada through the Book Publishing Industry Development Program (BPIDP) for our publishing activities.

National Library of Canada Cataloguing in Publication Data

Booth, David
   Reading & writing in the middle years

Includes bibliographical references and index.
ISBN 1-55138-136-2

1. Reading (Elementary)   2. Reading (Middle school)
3. English language—Composition and exercises—Study and teaching
(Elementary) 4. English language—Composition and exercises—Study
and teaching (Middle school)   I. Title.
II. Title: Reading and writing in the middle years.

LB1632.B66 2001   372.41'2   C2001-901389-2

Editor: Kat Mototsune
Cover Design: John Zehethofer
Cover Photo: PhotoDisc
Typesetting: Jay Tee Graphics

Printed and bound in Canada
9 8 7 6 5 4 3

INTRODUCTION

I no longer have my own class of children to teach—or should I say classes, since I spent much of my life working in a senior elementary school rotary system, where classes moved from room to room, carrying the bits and pieces of their lives with them through the halls.

For over two decades, I have worked at a faculty of education but, by a stroke of luck, our elementary program was based in project schools. The community of sixty student teachers and our staff team would meet and work each day in a school setting. As well, for two days each week the student teachers worked alongside teachers in their classrooms, learning about teaching from the inside out. This arrangement allowed me to spend a great deal of time in actual classrooms, sometimes demonstrating a particular teaching method with the student teachers, or setting up a literacy event that required the student teachers and the youngsters to work together on a unit of discovery. There were many times I was invited to visit an associate teacher's classroom to work with the children for an extended period of time, exploring a new book that required children to open up my understanding of its potential, or trying out techniques I had discovered while participating in a conference or from a new professional book that had intrigued me. The teachers who shared their classes with me are true professionals, eager to discover new ways of strengthening their teaching, and valuing the dozens of opportunities they found for observing their students in action.

Teaching graduate courses introduced me to other fine educators, who brought their teaching practice to their educational studies and created deep contexts for examining how and why we teach these students in the middle years. Many invited me to their classrooms, and my storehouse of authentic teaching anecdotes was replenished again and again. A teacher in New York once asked me, "How do you get to be good?" Her eyes were full of tears, and all I could answer was, "Hang around good people." That is what I have done throughout my professional life. This book could not exist without support from the teachers in the schools where I work, the colleagues in my faculty, the ideas I glean from educational researchers and writers. But I need to especially recognize the editors who have guided and supported me over the last thirty years. As I list their names, I am surprised by how many there are. The details are still clear in my mind, of our relationships as we struggled along together through dozens of books. Writing is such hard work, and when I consider those who have led me into a literate life, I am so grateful:

Stan Skinner, David Kilgour, Mary Macchiusi, Wendy Cochran, Diane Taylor, Cheryl Turner, Debbie Rogosin, Joanne Close, Marion Seary, Sheba Meland, Grant Heckman, Elizabeth Reid and all the others. My hope is that our students will be able to draw up a similar list by naming their teachers, those wise and gracious others who sat down beside them and talked about their work, who shared the craft of writing and supported their growth in the world of words and ideas.

You will notice throughout this book I have punctuated the text with excerpts from novels and poems from children's literature, bits and pieces about us, about school days and school teachers. The ability of authors and poets to show young people to see through us often scares me, but usually they peer into our hearts and forgive us our frailties. We can learn so much from the print artists who catch us, as a good photographer does, unawares.

For this book, I have called upon several teachers whose classes I know well, where I have spent time and have found opportunities to observe, teach and collect the samples of student work to illustrate my attempts at describing the strategies students use as proficient readers and writers:

Larry Swartz is an amazing teacher. He works in his classroom as well as with our faculty. His balancing of theory and practice makes his teaching invaluable to someone like me, who is in constant search for evidence of our professional strength. His classroom events have acted as a magic resource for many of my books, workshops and talks. His knowledge of books is endless, and he shares it with us all.

Nancy Steele taught my son in seventh grade. We both owe her mountains of gratitude, and her teaching shines even more brightly today. The writings from her middle-year students grow deeper and more artful each year.

Ken Wood has supported my work for the last seven years as my program assistant, and now he is a teacher. With his middle-year students, he has developed a framework for assessing their literacy growth and for helping them to assess their own development.

Gini Dickie teaches in an inner-city school that has been the centre for many of our student teachers. Her classroom appears to be filled with gifted children and, under her grand plan, that is just what they have become.

Michael Rossetti works with struggling readers in an urban secondary school, and he is tireless in his efforts to find effective stories for his students, as well as in encouraging them to write their own life tales.

There are countless other teachers and principals who invite me into their schools, who talk to me through letters and e-mails, who keep me engaged in the search for ways to increase my professionalism in education. As I write, I hear their voices.

ONE

Readers and Writers in the Middle Years

Different districts use different terms for organizing their school divisions. For the purposes of this book, the middle years include pre-adolescent and young adolescent students who are developing their own interests as readers and expanding their personal abilities as writers. Of course, these students will be in different stages of development while placed in one classroom: some are avid voluntary readers while others are still struggling; some write easily with good command of transcription skills while others lack confidence to put pencil to paper; some speak up in book discussions, eager to share their responses, while others draw back and remain silent. Most want to work independently, manage their own learning and follow their own interests. As they attempt to find their own voices, they discover the complexities of relationships and the tentative nature of their roles in a middle-school community.

The lives of these students are changing drastically, and these developments are reflected in both the content of what they read and in their attitudes toward writing. Family patterns are changing; young people are becoming more critical of parents, adults in authority and siblings; they depend more and more on peer groups, and have entertainment stars, sport heroes and friends as role models; future careers are talked about, and they begin to look forward to their own independence, testing their own positions at every stage. Many are developing a sense of history and of their own place in society; they are becoming concerned with justice and the unfair treatment of minority groups. Of course, their physical development is a central factor influencing their lives, relationships and identities.

Students who enter the middle years are expected to read and write independently and more often, to read longer and more difficult texts in a variety of curriculum areas, to read faster and more selectively, to write coherently with their own voices, to remember more information and to make integrated connections with the curriculum. There are new words and terms to learn in all of the different subject areas; some of the texts may be outdated, inaccessible or poorly written; readers of widely differing abilities are expected to read the same resources with few support structures. We want to encourage students in these classrooms to work responsibly together as a community. If we collaborate with them in negotiating how we will explore the curriculum as language learners, we can observe from the inside out how each student learns best and select our strategies carefully, so that young people do not spend their time attending to what they already know or pretending to be learning when they are completely lost.

When students feel the liberation that comes from having a say in what they read and write, they have a stake in creating and maintaining a classroom that stimulates and supports deep learning, freeing you as the teacher to concentrate on how you can best guide, inform and strengthen their abilities. I am necessary in my classroom: I know about the reading and writing processes; I have knowledge about how language works, the elements of craft that authors use, the pitfalls that young authors face; I know how to locate books that can lead to deeper thought. Sometimes I will tell my students things they need to know, but I have to balance those times with working alongside them, encouraging them in their beginning efforts, nudging them into richer texts, dialoguing with them about their stories and their research, reflecting and possibly illuminating their expanding worlds.

Literacy teaching is about honoring each student's potential as a developing reader and writer. We need to engage our students in intensive and extensive literacy events so that they can expand and refine both their ability to use language appropriately and effectively, and their knowledge about how oral and written communication works. In *When Writers Read* Jane Hanson says that they must read as writers and write as readers, going beyond the doing of the activity to a reflective awareness of all the different aspects of making meaning .

In his book *The Courage to Teach* Parker Palmer sums up this approach to teaching with these principles:

> A desire to help my students build a bridge between the academic text and their own lives and a strategic approach for doing so;
>
> A respect for my students' stories that is no more or less than my respect for the scholarly texts I assigned to them;
>
> An aptitude for asking good questions and listening carefully to my students' responses—not only to what they say but also to what they leave unsaid. (p. 82)

The noted educator James Moffett said more than thirty years ago that we need to make the solitary acts of reading and writing socially constructed events if we want to promote literacy development in young people. The "peer group imperative" demonstrated every day by our students may be our greatest classroom asset. There is such satisfaction in watching developing readers enter a discussion with a group about a shared selection, as they begin to notice how they create meaning, to wrestle with ideas, to prove a point by reading a portion of the text, to ask questions about the comments of group members, to draw inferences from the discussion and the words on the page and to gain insights from their own experiences with print. They are constructing meaning together, making sense of their own responses to what they have read and heard, mediated by the ideas and feeling of the group members. Suddenly reading has become an interactive process, a socially constructed learning experience.

We need to help students understand the different purposes for reading and writing, and give them strategies for making connections between the texts they read and texts they construct. We need to place our teaching of reading and writing inside events that require actual and authentic reading and writing, instead of simply evaluating them after the fact.

My role as a teacher is complex and changing:

I need to lead but I need to respond.

I need to inform but I need to listen.

I need to instruct but I need to collaborate.

I need to evaluate but I need to teach.

I need to demonstrate but I need to participate.

I need to organize but I need to become involved.

I need to manage but I need to support.

I need to model but I need to assist.

I need to confer but I need to observe.

I need to criticize but I need to appreciate.

One day while walking along the street with my friend Doug, he murmured aloud, "Isn't it wonderful to be in the centre of the city and to be able to see the lake?"

I turned to him and asked "What are you talking about?"

"Look up," Doug told me, and I did, and I saw the water on the horizon. All those years of walking on Yonge Street, and I thought the lake was too far away to consider. Yet there it was, in full view. I must let friends like Doug teach me how to see what I have never seen, to learn from those who see more clearly than I ever thought I could. We can teach and we can learn.

- We need to understand and appreciate the developing characteristics and behaviors of individual students in the middle years in our classrooms.
- We need to strive to create in school a literacy community for our students that connects to their homes and to their outside worlds, so that we can support them in becoming independent and life-long readers and writers.
- We need to help our students move towards becoming responsible for their own learning, capable of making choices and taking action, and able to handle some of the challenges and problems in their lives.
- We need to model literacy by sharing experiences from our own lives as readers and writers, and by demonstrating techniques and strategies for our students so that they can grow as literate beings.
- We need to provide our students with a wide variety of resources that they want to read, and at different reading levels that they can read.
- We need to encourage our students to connect the texts they read to their personal experiences, to their feelings and to past and present world events.
- We need to develop authentic reasons for having our students write, so they will have opportunities to write for a variety of functions and for different audiences.
- We need to provide explicit instruction in reading and writing, so that all our students can acquire the strategies that will help them to read and write more complex and meaningful texts.
- We need to support our students in their reading and writing in a variety of genres and text structures found across the curriculum.
- We need to develop assessment strategies and use evaluation procedures to enable our students to recognize their strengths and uncover their problems, so that we can design useful instruction for supporting their literacy growth.
- We need to continue to grow as professionals in our teaching: questioning and reflecting upon our own practice as well as the policies and the curricula we follow; reading about the classroom discoveries of other educators in new books and journal articles; attending in-service sessions and conferences as both leaders and participants, and living our lives as involved and participating readers and writers.

Teaching Reading

I remember years ago observing a colleague as she taught a novel, watching her hammer out with her class what seemed like hundreds of insignificant details that no reader would be able to notice or remember. I later asked her about her work with this particular book, and she told me that her students had to know the novel backwards and forwards. But when I mentioned that schools and classrooms in her city were reading and teaching different novels, she stared at me, wondering aloud how those youngsters would learn about the book she had chosen. And, of course, she soon came to realize that they would all find different books in their lives, and that how they made sense of them would depend on the strategies that we helped them to develop. We certainly don't share a book as a cultural symbol in our learning communities in order to remember irrelevant data. There must be better reasons for reading and reflecting upon shared texts in our classrooms.

Many of us began our careers feeling ill-prepared as literacy teachers, and it is not surprising that we often have students perform on demand, instead of finding ways to help them learn about the processes of reading and writing. We know that evaluation is not teaching but, if we are constantly using testing situations in lieu of methodology, how will our struggling readers grow? We need to reconsider our roles as literacy teachers, to discover with our students the strategies that work and to select interesting, worthwhile and significant resources to read and write about. As teaching professionals, we often feel like the character Miss Narwin in Avi's *Nothing but the Truth*, who no longer could cope with the pressures of teaching, and retires and moves to Florida.

> Mr. Duval, as I see it, I have been working—working hard — as a teacher for twenty years. I've been a good teacher. Ask my principal if that's not so. Do you know, she was once my student.

I have decided to relax about the huge numbers of curriculum guidelines, educational outcomes, assessment targets, reporting procedures, teacher evaluations, government directives and research projects. Every state, every province, every district, and almost every school has a committee drawing up documents outlining every skill and achievement outcome under the sun. Hurray! Now that we all know what we are supposed to do, we can be grateful for all that information and focus on the art of teaching. For, in the end, it is the human interaction in our classrooms that will determine what children will learn and what children will remember. The stories they tell to their grandchildren will be about us.

As teachers, we can model our own literacy with our students as often as possible. We all remember a teacher who read us a letter she had received or an editorial from a newspaper about an issue she cared deeply about, who showed us the novel she was reading or the information books she had found about her hobby. My high-school algebra teacher would try to solve the math puzzle from the morning newspaper on the blackboard before our class began. He loved his discipline, and told stories of how he used it as a fighter pilot during World War II. I remember him forty years later.

The teachers in my graduate courses write about their literacy lives, and I am often moved by their recollections of their parents, of the struggles of some immigrant families who couldn't read in English, of homes where books were either invisible or sacred, or where book learning was the only way to open doors. I hope that teachers will share their life tales about literacy with their students, so that we uncover the hidden truths and eliminate the often elitist trappings of the myth-filled phenomenon called reading.

Recently, I e-mailed my friend Meguido Zola, who teaches at Simon Fraser University, and asked him what he was reading. Here's his answer:

> My recreational reading tends, these days, to focus on "reading sign" as Native Americans have called it; on "reading the book of the world," to use the language of mediaeval Catholic monks.
>
> As I (re)read Parker Palmer's *Let Your Life Speak: Listening for the Voice of Vocation*, I am trying to make better sense of my life, to find more meaning in the signs written in the texts of my life's experiences.
>
> At the same time, I'm slowly making my way through Richard Stone's *The Healing Art of Storytelling*, which is helping me search for the maps that connect the many disparate paths I have traveled: this will help me shed light on my past and help me complete a circle by connecting the past to my "current concerns, feelings, needs, aspirations, and outlook." In this way, Stone encourages me, I may discover more of my truth—at least for now.
>
> As I'm readying myself for a month's walking holiday in the Cotswolds in England, I'm also reading Joseph Dispenza's *The Way of the Traveler*, which tells me there is only one journey—going inside yourself. Also, by my bedside, is Phil Cousineau's *The Art of Pilgrimage*, a text I read again each summer: it similarly instructs me how to travel outwards to the edges of the world while at the same time journeying to the depths of my soul. Every journey can be transformative if it is undertaken with a desire for spiritual risk and renewal...and that's how I like it!
>
> So, you see, I have many books on the go at the same time: some, I'm reading for the first time; others I'm rereading. Some, I read all the way through; others, at a leisurely pace, perhaps pausing to meditate upon and respond to in writing; yet others, only in fits and starts, as the mood takes me. My reading flows out of whatever happen to be my current interests and concerns—and, while some of these remain constant (spirituality), others are seasonal (travel), and yet others only fleeting and transitory.

I am very fortunate in having so much literary support in my friends, as they share books and articles they are reading: Kathleen slips a newspaper article about single-sex schools under my office door; Larry puts a new picture book by Anthony Browne in my mailbox; Suzanne surprises me with a new book on arts education she has ordered for me online; Bob tells me about a new British poetry book that has delighted him; Marion writes from England mentioning three books on education I need to buy; Stan phones to tell me of an article in the *New Yorker* I must read. I need these networks to strengthen and enrich my literacy life. We all need support from the teacher down the hall, colleagues in other schools, friends online, students, parents, consultants and reviewers. And so do our students.

✓ We need to talk about the reading in our students' lives, so that we can find out what they think about their reading: their questions, reactions, interpretations, opinions, inferences, arguments and celebrations.

✓ If we belong to a book club, we can share some of the proceedings with our students: How are the books selected? Who decides what we will talk about? When do we find time to read the books? How do we make sense of the books we are reading? How do we notice our own use of the reading strategies?

✓ If we are taking a course ourselves, we can show our students the texts and articles we are using, revealing our own modes of sorting, marking or highlighting texts.

✓ We need to model how we think when we read real texts through frequent classroom demonstrations, so that students see inside the process of understanding how print works. I want my students to notice me as a reader and a writer, how I function within the culture of literacy. I want to be aware of my own thinking and strategies with print, how I handle my own confusion and breakdowns when I read, and my own stops and starts when I write. In *Dialogic Inquiry* Gordon Wells says, "Learning to be literate can be thought of as an intellectual apprenticeship" (p. 164).

Constructing Meaning

Meaning-making with print is developmental and can expand exponentially over time, if we have wise others to support us. Students need to be located in the company of those who are considering similar issues and ideas generated by the text—classmates, critics and reviewers, teachers who share and direct their learning, other authors whose writing connects to their work and references that add to their background knowledge. The landscape of our minds is constantly shifting as we read and reflect on what we have read. Our comprehension alters as our life goes on, as we consider the ideas and opinions of others. Our response to a single text is never frozen in time.

Reading, of course, is more than pronouncing words; it is more than attempting to second guess the intent of the author. It is a process of interpretation and negotiation from the locus of our lived and vicarious experiences at a moment in time. We need to constantly expand our abilities to process print, from a single word on a billboard to a dense novel translated from the Russian. Texts will continue to present challenges to us for the rest of our reading lives—the words, the language patterns, the structure and organization, our purpose for reading a particular text and, especially, the connections we make.

The reader is part writer; a book is like a printed circuit that the reader's life flows through. The text furnishes the hints, the clues, the framework, and the reader constructs the meaning. The reader writes the story by bringing self to the print, engaging with the text to create a thoughtful and mindful experience. Comprehension is now viewed as a complex process involving background knowledge, personal experience, thinking processes and responses. Reading shapes and even changes our thinking; reading is thinking.

Some students tell us that they can read the words in the text but they don't seem to understand what they read. To become insightful readers, they will need to extend their thinking beyond a superficial understanding of the text. As readers, we need to acquire knowledge, explain information, connect it to previous knowledge and then use it in some way. We need to think about not only what we are reading, but what we are learning. As we read, we want to build up our store of knowledge, develop insight, think more deeply and critically, question, interpret and evaluate what we are reading. We construct our own meaning as we make connections, ask questions, make inferences, select important ideas and synthesize our learning. We use the text to stimulate our own thinking so we can engage with the mind of the writer.

How do we help those readers in the middle years who think reading is pronouncing words rather than making meaning with the text? Are we, as teachers, following an unwritten and sequenced curriculum of literacy that seems to say, "Learn words in the primary years, find main ideas and details in the junior years, and examine author intent for the rest of your school lives"? How is it possible for youngsters to have success in school without thinking deeply and struggling to construct meaning with what they read? Yet even authors such as Bill Martin Jr. and David Bouchard tell us they did exactly that. In her book *I Read It, But I Don't Get It*, Cris Tovani describes these students as fake-readers, people who made their way through school by pretending they could read, disguising their limitations, using their listening skills and powers of memory to make up for not being able to handle print. They had no intellectual involvement with the text; they relied on the teacher's summaries or on copying what others said; they quickly grew frustrated by a lengthy or complex selection, waiting for the teacher to tell them what to think.

However, non-readers, unmotivated readers, reluctant readers and limited readers can all grow with the right set of conditions. We know stories from those who work with adult illiterates how their students eventually, and with support, come to be print powerful. We hear, from teachers who work with youngsters in remedial reading classes, of the great strides many students make with guidance and instruction. And we listen to the stories of those who struggled with reading—some of them teachers and writers—who, with the help of someone who understood the reading process, gained membership in what Frank Smith called the literacy club.

When readers develop strategies for understanding different texts and for monitoring their own reading, they are on their way to becoming fluent, independent readers who can assume control and responsibility for their learning. Along the way, they need secure environments in which they can experience plenty of success in their reading ventures, where they feel safe to experiment and make and modify errors or miscues in their reading. They need to take charge of their own development as readers.

READING GOALS FOR STUDENTS

- Participate in a variety of reading/listening experiences each day.
- Read a variety of genres in different formats.
- Learn to choose books independently and appropriately.
- Read silently for an intensive and sustained period each day.
- Read common texts with other group members.
- Reflect on and respond to what you read.
- Have conversations with classmates and the teacher about what you read.
- Recommend books you have read to others.
- Keep a reading journal for recording your books and your responses.
- Become familiar with authors and illustrators that you appreciate.
- Notice what your teacher chooses to read.
- Develop your own preferences for reading materials.
- Read critically, being mindful and thoughtful of the connections you are making.
- Continue to expand your repertoire of reading strategies.
- Apply your knowledge of reading in all subject areas.
- Participate in a variety of read-aloud activities, including shared reading and community reading.
- See yourself as a successful reader in your literacy community.

Teaching Writing

When I began teaching, I scheduled creative writing for Tuesdays at two o'clock, ignoring the fact that students were writing throughout the day in various curriculum subjects. Revision and editing were demanded, but instruction was seldom offered. I chose each topic for all the students to address, and I waited for them to be finished. Sometimes I provided a prompt for a student staring at a blank page but, on the whole, I ran a performance-based program, where students completed a first draft and then wrote a good copy that I would mark. What was missing, I now know, was any understanding of the writer's work, of the writing process and of the strategies that might be of help to developing student authors.

Fortunately, the English consultant, Bill Moore, visited my classroom and demonstrated many times with my students a variety of writing strategies; after each visit, I revised my own teaching repertoire and my understanding of the role of a writing teacher. He gave me my first two professional books: *Creative Power* by Hughes Mearns, published in 1929, was a narrative account of his work with teachers on writing—I marveled at this author's sensitivity and compassion for the struggles teachers go through in finding purposes for students to write; the other book was *When the Teacher Says, "Write a Poem"* by Mauree Applegate, an American educator who conducted radio shows that motivated students to write with vigor and joy. She wrote the line that altered my work forever: "When we correct their work with red pens, we cut across their lives with a scalpel, drawing blood."

Of course, today we have in our professional collections books by educators who have studied, taught and reflected upon how writers write, and we can use those models to create classroom programs that nurture and teach youngsters to write like writers. I am grateful to the educators who began examining the writing process, researching and reflecting on how we might begin to support our students: Donald Graves, Lucy Calkins, Shelley Harwayne, Mary Ellen Giacobbi, Nancie Atwell, Ralph Fletcher and so many others. We now have a body of work that can inform our teaching and offer us methods and inspiration, strategies for assisting developing young writers as well as information about the writer's craft.

I write collaboratively with my students who are studying to be teachers; I talk out loud in front of them using transparencies and charts, revealing how I revise and rethink my work as it develops, make decisions, edit the conventions—how I write down my life. I share my writing: letters, stories, vignettes, memoirs, summaries, reviews and reports. I want the students to see me as a developing writer who understands what and why he teaches. I have my memory of Bill Moore beside me every step of the way: he wrote on the blackboard throughout the lesson, his poems and students' poems, interactively editing with the students, and they recognized his strengths and took understanding from his process. He was a reciprocal teacher, and I stared in awe.

We must never forget that the students are surrounded by demonstrations, both implicit and explicit, of attitudes and behaviors concerning reading and writing. The gym teacher who made fun of the USSR at one of my schools left the wrong impression with the students, that jocks don't read or appreciate those who do.

Quality writing occurs in a classroom where students write about things that matter to them, where a language-rich, supportive environment fosters their desire to see themselves as writers and increases their ability to capture their ideas and feelings proficiently. We want youngsters to have real purposes for writing, to speak in their own voices with clarity and accuracy. Writing may not be easy or fun, but it can be satisfying and purposeful, an important aspect of living. Think about what we can do as writers: think in print, brainstorm ideas and observations, scribble down our thoughts, test ideas, ponder our problems, record and plan our lives. We record disjointed thoughts, ask questions, move around ideas, organize our bits and pieces and surprise ourselves with our discoveries. And occasionally we communicate our writing in a permanent form with others, personally or professionally. Often we don't know what we really think until we try to write it down.

For some of us, writing brings back difficult memories of red-covered edits, failing grades, mandatory topics of little interest. The only audience was the instructor, who seldom found our ideas interesting. And then we find ourselves teaching writing to a class of students. How can we change our writing backgrounds and become professional, knowledgeable and literate writing teachers? One way is to begin behaving as writers ourselves and helping students to act as real writers who write because they have something they want to say.

My colleague Shelley Peterson is exploring gender influences on adolescent students' writing choices, and on teachers' assessment of student writing. Her research (1998) shows that teachers perceive girls to be better writers than boys. In one instance in an Alberta study, these perceptions led to a significant bias in teachers' evaluations of a sample of student narrative writing. Questioning the degree of objectivity possible in writing assessment when teachers' gender expectations are ignored or suppressed, she advocates bringing these expectations to a conscious level and examining the evaluation criteria for gender biases.

In Shelley's research, participating students also perceived girls to be better writers than boys. Their perception that writing revealed information about the sexual identity of the writer limited their choices of topics, characters and genres. Adolescent boys, in particular, wrote with the awareness that disrupting a taken-for-granted gender order by writing in ways that were typically associated with girls would result in negative social consequences. Shelley proposes that encouraging students to deconstruct gender meanings in their own writing and teaching mini-lessons on skills for social change, such as supporting students who explore non-stereotypical gender meanings in their writing, are starting points for expanding the choices that students make while writing.

We need to have our students writing frequently during the day in a variety of situations: note-taking during a mini-lesson; working on an idea web for a social studies project; completing a final draft of an extended independent piece. But only the last example requires extensive editing; we publish our writing when we have something special to share and to keep. We can consider the act of writing like other functions of communication, such as talk: sometimes we chat with strangers, argue with our boss, present a formal proposal to our colleagues, talk to ourselves in the car on the way home, whisper to our partner in bed.

Developing as a writer is a life-long journey. Every time I am involved in a writing project, I learn. Our knowledge of the writing process grows and builds over time, and each year can contribute to students' developing abilities to construct ideas and feelings with words, confidently and competently, so they can share their creations with others. A student's writing growth over several years is observable in the accumulated writing samples, record and progress sheets and teacher comments. We can gain professional satisfaction from this evidence of their ongoing journeys.

WRITING GOALS FOR STUDENTS

- Write each day for a variety of purposes.
- Keep a writer's notebook and gather and collect observations and ideas for future writing projects.
- Record your own feelings and experiences.
- Choose most of your topics for your writing projects.
- Write in a variety of genres.
- Use different formats for different projects.
- Learn about the craft of writing from noticing how authors work.
- Develop the skills of revision and editing.
- Learn more about how words and sentences work.
- Participate in conferences with the teacher and other students.
- Share your writing with your classmates and listen to and read theirs.
- Use writing as a tool for thinking and reflecting out loud.
- Communicate with others through writing.
- See yourself as writer in other areas of the curriculum.
- Request feedback from others in planning and revising your writing.
- Keep the audience in mind when you are writing.
- Incorporate the computer into your writing projects.
- Keep a writing folder for your projects.
- Publish a writing project each month.

Reading Strategies

What if we based our teaching on sharing the strategies that proficient readers use to comprehend text—showing our students how to think deeply about what they read as they read, helping them move beyond the superficial so they can discover their own ability to understand, to reflect about what they have met in print and to move towards the insight that comes from connecting and considering their connections to the text?

Proficient readers use reading strategies to build meaning and comprehend text automatically and seamlessly as they work in real reading situations. However, we need to support all students in becoming readers who have strategies for overcoming difficulties they encounter instead of pretending or giving up on a text. Explicit instruction through mini-lessons and demonstrations can clarify procedures for them and enhance their abilities to work with texts.

As students grow comfortable using a particular strategy, we can ask them to write about how the strategy works and how it helps their reading. The act of writing about it can make the strategy concrete for the students and allow them to move forward to include other strategies in their own reading. Today while reading the newspaper, I made a miscue that startled me: instead of "Basketball star signing with Raptors," I misread the word as "singing," and couldn't make sense of what was going on until I reread it. We can keep a list of the miscues we all make when we read, and celebrate our abilities as readers to fix print that doesn't make sense.

Strategies and processes are, to a large extent, intangible. Because of this, we can never be certain how students employ them. Instead, we need to watch for evidence of specific strategy use, and notice the degree of success students meet when using them.

Proficient readers are those who

- understand the purpose for reading a particular text
- overview the text by skimming and scanning it
- use the features of the text to understand how it is organized

- activate their background knowledge to make sense of the text
- attempt to anticipate the events in the text
- process print with fluency, using punctuation and phrasing
- maintain a consistent focus on constructing meaning
- monitor and repair comprehension throughout the reading process
- recognize a large number of words automatically
- solve unfamiliar words using a variety of strategies while reading for meaning
- connect text to self, text to text, and text to world
- recognize and prioritize important ideas
- have questions in mind before, during and after the reading
- draw inferences during and after the reading
- summarize and synthesize information during and after reading
- visualize pictures in the mind while reading
- respond to text in order to reexamine, modify and extend meaning making

Thinking as We Read

We can find hundreds of texts and articles written over the last fifty years that list thinking skills for us, from Bloom's taxonomy to every contemporary college text on reading. But for me, the turnaround came in the early seventies with James Moffett's text *Student-Centered Language Arts and Reading K–12*, when he explained how these thinking processes had been misappropriated by educators and labeled as reading skills. Thinking operations occur in our responses to all the texts we experience in our lives—conversations, films, books, magazines, tapes and CDs. Nevertheless, helping students to become aware of the relationship of thought and print the texts they meet is vital to their growth as readers. A friend, about to embark on a canoeing trip in the north, asked his father if he knew someone who could accompany them, someone who could "read rivers." There are many literacies. They all involve reading.

Making Connections

My son came home from grade nine excited about his history class: "Dad, did you know that Caesar is not just a salad?" Now we laugh together at that memory, but the incident highlights how we can only recognize what we have somehow met before. Our knowledge is built from and based on all we have experienced, and those connections are being made all the time, consciously and subconsciously.

For example, when we are engaged with a book, we bring the sum total of our life to the meaning-making experience: our previous experiences; our background knowledge concerning the content; our connections to other "texts of our lives," the books, computer programs or songs that are suddenly conjured up; our emotional frame; our knowledge of the nature of this particular text—how it works, the author's style; and the events of the world at large that are somehow triggered or referenced by our reading. A great deal is happening in a reader's mind.

The British poet Ted Hughes reminds us that the word *crucifixion* contains 2000 years of history. When we are engaged in the act of reading, connections are occurring constantly and simultaneously as we recall personal experiences, summarize what has happened so far, synthesize information and add it to our constantly expanding mental storehouse, analyze and challenge the author's ideas, and change the organizational schema of our minds. Making connections with what we read is a complex process. When we instruct students to notice, for example, only the words in a text without considering meaning, we are eliminating all the other mental connections that educate us as readers; we limit the use of the construct the brain has created to handle incoming data for processing.

Our main goal as literacy teachers must be to help students build bridges between the ideas in the text and their own lives, helping them to access the prior knowledge that is relevant to making meaning with the text, the information that the brain has retained and remembered, sometimes accompanied by emotional responses or visual images. When we help students enhance their reading by activating their own connections, we offer them a reading strategy for life.

These connections have been classified as text to self (connecting to past experiences and background), text to text (connecting to other texts in our lives and to the forms those texts take), and text to world (connecting to events in the world at large). As the three general categories interconnect and intersect, students have a strategy for coming at a text selection in a variety of ways. As they begin to observe and reflect upon how these connections affect their understanding of a particular text, they can deliberately use each aspect of the connection frame to increase their personal and collective processes of meaning making.

In their book *Strategies that Work*, Stephanie Harvey and Anne Goudvis remind us that "students may need to be shown how to make meaningful rather that tangential connections with the text" (p. 77). All kinds of connections whiz through our minds as we read a text, and these can lead to fascinating explorations, but generally we want to model and support those that promote deeper insights into our understanding of what we have been reading. However, even leftover reminiscences and queries may prove to be powerful resources if recorded in response journals during the reading workshop, where they can be developed and extended into thoughtful writing events.

Life Connections

I usually begin this strategy by sharing memoirs that remind students of personal experiences they may have had. I enjoy reading aloud Cynthia Rylant's *The Relatives Came.* I model my own connections, usually stopping at each page to share my own stories, and before long the hands go up as the students relate their own. We can in this way demonstrate that making connections needs to happen as we read, so that we are constantly expanding and processing different types of knowledge.

✓ During a demonstration with a shared selection, we can list the connections that everyone is making on a chart, and then label them by type. At the conclusion of the mini-lesson, the students can select a specific connection and develop it in their writing notebooks. This would be a good opportunity for the teacher to write as well, and model the process by sharing a connecting anecdote.

✓ Before the students begin to read, we can elicit what they already know about the topic or the theme of the book, and list their ideas on a mind-mapping web or a chart. Through guided discussion, we can prompt them to see that they do have connections to call upon that will support their reading—events from their own lives, bits of information gleaned from previous experiences with television or magazines, or stories they have heard from friends and relatives. The more prior knowledge we can tap into, the greater the meaning-making that will occur when we read.

✓ We can show the students how to code their responses while reading by having them mark the text with stick-it notes whenever they make a connection. These notes can form the basis for a discussion where students articulate their connections and begin to notice how our reading minds function. We need to help students understand how each connection relates to the text, and how it deepens or extends their understanding.

Maxine Bone and Susan Schwartz have articulated their construct of connecting in their book *Retelling, Relating, Reflecting.* We might say as we work, for example,

- This reminds me of…
- I remember when…
- It makes me think of…
- It makes me feel that…
- That happened to me, too, when…

- When I was young…
- That situation is just like…
- This is different from…
- This compares to…
- It sounds like…

Text Connections

We can help students begin to recognize text connections by selecting particular text sets to be used during independent reading or literature circles: books related by common themes or writing styles; books about the same characters or events; several books by the same author or from a particular genre; different versions of the same story. Comparisons and contrasts offer us a simple means of noting text-to-text connections. As students see other relationships among texts, we can record these on a chart as a reminder to make connections as they read.

Often students remember and bring forward past text experiences to clarify or substantiate a present discussion. They reveal that they are using text-to-text connections for deeper learning, tying what they have met before to what they are presently exploring and expanding their literacy perspectives. We can, of course, model this with our own comments during a class discussion.

During a reading time with three hundred students organized for an author celebration in a school library, I had chosen to read *The Seal Mother*. After the story, I casually asked if they knew other stories about foundlings or changelings, and one by one they offered tales they had met in their young experiences—of babies found in tree stumps, in bushes, in shells, in leaves—filling the room with story memories and increasing their knowledge of how folklore has worked for hundreds of years. I remember how the teachers beamed, proud of the connections their students were making, and of the story heritage so evident in that library.

By drawing attention to the features of different types of print texts, we can help our students understand how texts work, the nature of different genres, and the cues and literary features of each. The more familiar they are with the characteristics of a text, the more accessible it will become, and the more easily they will be able to read it. They will know what to expect when they read a novel, a science text, a poem or a letter; they will recognize the intent of a speech, an editorial or an article; they will know how a particular author such as Gary Paulsen structures a novel and why a narrative can be told through letters. I remember when a grade-six class in Vancouver told me, after they had read *Dear Mr. Henshaw* by Beverly Cleary, that it really wasn't a novel, just a series of letters. It was a great opportunity to talk about different formats that novelists can use to tell their stories.

World Connections

In my own work in the teaching of reading strategies, I am seldom satisfied unless the learning stretches outside the classroom lives of the students, connecting our reading to bigger world issues so that perspectives and assumptions are challenged or altered. I am grateful to Paulo Freire for giving us the expression "reading the word, reading the world." Somehow, when we read powerful, significant texts, we travel outside ourselves, exploring what lies beyond our immediate neighborhood, extending our vision and encouraging our personal meaning-making.

A grade-eight class was preparing to read *Tales from Gold Mountain* by Paul Yee, and I asked them who had built the railway across Canada. Several students agreed that it was the Germans and, when I asked why, they talked about the industrial force of that country and linked it with the world of giant steam trains. When I told them that Chinese boys, not much older than they were, had been used as laborers, they were completely surprised, and moved into the book with a very different mind set. One of the students captured her learning in her fictional diary:

Day 1
This is my first day in Canada after spending 14 days on the ship that brought me to my new life in Canada. We arrived in British Columbia, which is a province of Canada. I am just waiting for the ferry to come and take me to the part of the railway that I am going to be working at. I have waited many hours so far and there is still no sign of it coming. I am very hungry because the food that we received on the ship was not good at all. I hope that they will feed us better when we are working on the railroad. So far I think that I have made the right decision coming to Canada so that I can make some money to send back to my family in China.

Day 2
They took me to this shack and it was filled with all of the other Chinese workers. It is morning now so we are all waiting out by the docks for the ferry to come. In the distance we see the big stern wheeler coming towards us. As soon as it got to the docks we all got on the ferry and it took us to our destination. On our trip I have seen many animals and few people. This country is so different from the one that I come from. It seems that everyone here has money and a place to live but in China many people have nothing and no place to live.

It took us all day to get to the part of the railroad that we will be building. It is night time now and the only thing that I can see are tents and a few workers. We were shown to our beds which are in the tents. I thought that we would have been living in buildings rather than tents. They gave us dinner but it was only rice and dried fish. It wasn't much better than got on the ship coming here. I am already missing my family.

This student wrote dozens of entries in her fictional diary, incorporating the incidents and information that had arisen in the drama explorations. She created a world unlike her own but full of her own responses, writing inside an "as if" context, and "living through" those times inside her imagination. This kind of authentic writing represents narrative retellings, reflection and informational writing, all within one mode—writing generated by the role playing.

Questioning the Text

We read because we are curious about what we will find; we keep reading because of the questions that continue to fill our reading minds. Of course, readers ask questions before they read, as they read and when they are finished. As we become engaged with a text, questions keep popping up, questions that propel us to predict what will happen next, to challenge the author, to wonder about the context for what is happening, to fit the new information into our world picture. We try to rectify our confusion, filling in missing details, attempting to fit into a pattern all the bits and pieces that float around our sphere of meaning-making. We continue to read because the author has made us curious, and this constant self-questioning causes us to interact with the text, consciously and subconsciously. As we read on, our questions may change, and the answers we seek may lie outside the print.

The deeper and more complex the text, the more questions we will bring forward as we try to make sense of it. The greater our interest in what we are reading, the more substantive our questions will be. Monitoring our reading means paying attention to those questions that arise as we read, as well as those that remain when we are finished. We begin to make our connections to what we already know, wrinkling our brows at incongruities or seeming inconsistencies, accepting that our minds work in this inquiry method while we read, and that the questions that remain after the reading can form the basis for our text talk, for exploring further research or for just pondering and wondering about the complex issues that the reading has conjured up.

Often our most limited readers ask themselves the fewest questions as they read, waiting for us to interrogate them when they have finished the disenfranchising ritual of the prescribed print offering. They have not learned that confusion is allowed as we read, that in fact authors count on it in order to build the dynamic that compels us to continue reading. And as students grow in their ability to self-question, their understanding of how authors think and of how meaning-makers work increases.

How can we help youngsters interact with the text as they read, to care about what they are reading and to become engaged with the meaning-making that real reading requires?

✓ We can begin by showing how we ask questions ourselves throughout the reading experience, demonstrating the process and writing down the questions that come up in a selection we are sharing. This public monitoring of our own reading can often help student readers recognize how interacting with text works, and it may even free some of them from their own restrictive patterns of regarding the text as a frozen maze that seems unsolvable.

✓ If we introduce students to this inquiry-based mode of reading, they too can demonstrate their own self-questioning strategies. We can begin with a shared selection to read aloud, by using copies or working with the overhead projector. Students can use stick-it notes on their copies to note their questions as they read. After they have completed the text, we can categorize the questions according to type:
— questions that were answered as we read further
— questions that can be answered through inferences as we make other connections
— questions that simply cause us to wonder

Student-Generated Questions

We have a much greater chance of having our students invest themselves in the reading experience if we help them to take ownership with their own questions. They may begin to participate in the text-generated meaning-making if they believe that their questions really matter and that others are interested in grappling with them. Those who are wondering why they are not making sense of text might begin using their own questions to move them forward as they seek answers, information, or at least clarification. They read as real readers do, moving back and forth between their own lives and the worlds created by the author, wondering, pondering, challenging, inquiring, rereading, searching, summarizing and always questioning. It is the way humans learn, and the way readers read.

Student-generated questions may lead to deeper comprehension when students can give voice to their own concerns. Cris Tovani in her book *I Read It,*

But I Don't Get It says, "Forging paths of new thinking is discouraged when students aren't allowed to cultivate uncertainties" (p. 81). Struggling readers can begin to take control over their own reading as they raise questions that matter to them and search for answers both inside and outside the text.

I enjoy using the picture book *The King's Fountain* by Lloyd Alexander as a medium for examining this strategy with students of all ages. The story concerns a king who decides to build a fountain that would use up all the water in the village. An impoverished old man finally persuades the ruler not to carry out his plan. As I read it aloud, the participants record their questions. When I have finished reading, we take time to classify the questions in order to see where their interests lie. This helps me to know which direction to take, as together we explore the issues in the story:

- Why were there no female adults portrayed in the story?
- Why did the village rely upon a single source of water for its very life?
- What were the king's true motives in building this fountain?
- Is there another way the king could show his glory to the people?
- What was so intimidating about the king that no one would approach him?
- Had an event like the building of the fountain happened in the past?
- What happened in the king's past that made him think that it was appropriate to take away the village's water?
- How did the villagers earn their livelihoods?
- Why was the old man chosen to go to the king? (Were there no village advisors? No council?)
- What did the girl say to inspire her father to speak with the king?

Teacher-Generated Questions

When I go to a teachers' conference and see dozens of manuals filled with questions for studying *Charlotte's Web*, my heart sinks. How will we ever help young readers become independent thinkers who will choose to engage with a text, if we don't allow them to predict as they read, to practice inferential thinking, to question the text? When will they learn to draw their own conclusions, to seek out further information, to ask a friend for an opinion on a difficult issue that arises? How will they learn to become curious about the ideas generated by the author? What if those guides and question sheets are demonstrating for students that someone else always decides what is important in their reading and writing, and that they will never need to take control of their own literacy needs, never make responsible decisions for how to progress in their learning? And my guilt-ridden teacher voice asks, "Why did I spend so much of my teaching life inventing questions, when the students might have brought forward much better ones?"

Lists of predigested and impersonal comprehension questions are no longer part of my life or my classroom teaching. However, published programs often offer me ideas for giving the students thoughtful and deepening literacy strategies, for suggesting book sets to increase the reading repertoires of the students, or for presenting significant background information to support the text.

Of course, I have questions to ask, but they will grow from conversations with the text, from the honest revelations of the students' own concerns, as I try to guide them into deeper interpretations. Now I attempt to ask questions driven by our inquiring dialogue, as I would in a conversation with peers during a book-club session, based on my listening to their interactions rather than on my own scripted agenda. I want students to engage in thoughtful considerations about the text and its connections to their lives, not struggle to find the responses they think I want. I like the description Gay Su Pinnell and Irene Fountas give in their book *Guiding Readers and Writers* for using this strategy: "The teacher's questions are a light scaffold that helps students examine text in new ways" (p. 294).

We can model and demonstrate how effective questions work, showing the need to listen carefully to others, revisiting points in the text that support a particular comment and supporting effective responses of the students.

✓ Try asking no questions during a text discussion, but note down the ones you might have asked in the past. Or record a text talk session between you and the students, and play it back to analyze the types of questions you used and the effect on your students' contributions.

✓ Rather than initiating questions, build on the questions and comments of the students by offering open-ended responses after they speak, encouraging further contributions and helping to focus and deepen the dialogue.

✓ Consider using prompts rather than recall questions in your interactions with students during group sessions and individual conferences, and in your responses to their reading and writing journals. These prompts can expand or deepen the offerings of the students, help them clarify or expand their thoughts and nudge them into expressing their opinions and ideas. We have questions to ask and we need to ask them, but we want to teach our students to ask their own as well.

✓ Separate assessment questions from your text discussions. If you clearly state the purpose of the evaluation activity, whether in practice sessions or in a testing situation, it can help students understand the difference purposes of each and to learn how to handle both types of events.

Making Inferences

We spend our life making inferences, noting all the signs that help us to make sense of any experience—the face of the salesclerk displaying a product, week-end weather reports, the body language of the students we are teaching. As readers or viewers, we make inferences when we go beyond the literal meaning of the text—whether it is a film, a speech or a book—and begin to examine the implied meanings, reading between the lines to hypothesize what the author intended, what he or she was really trying to say and why. When we read, our connections drive us to infer; we struggle to make sense of the text, looking into our minds to explain what isn't on the page, building theories that are more than just the words. We conjecture while we are reading, the information accrues, our ideas are modified, changed or expanded as this new text enters the constructs in our brain. Inferencing allows us to activate our connections at deeper levels, and to negotiate and wonder until further information confirms or expands our initial meaning-making ventures. Predictions are inferences that are usually confirmed or altered, but most inferences are open-ended, unresolved, adding to the matrix of our connections. Often we need to dialogue with others to further explore these expanding thoughts, and to become more adept at recognizing the need for digging deeply into the ideas of the text.

I presented a senior high-school class with a rhyme to interpret:

> Old Abram Brown is dead and gone,
> You'll never see him more;
> He used to wear a long brown coat
> That buttoned down before.

I provided no information, not even the clue that the poem was from Mother Goose. Without discussion, the students read and wrote down their impressions. Their comments reveal much about the inferences they made based upon their past experiences.

> He was just an ordinary man. There was nothing special about him. Instead of commenting on a great achievement in the man's life, or on a particular noteworthy characteristic that he may have possessed, the author decides to remember the man by his coat. This might be because the author didn't know anything more about Abram Brown, or maybe there was nothing more significant about Abram Brown's life that was worth commenting on.

> It reminded me of how I felt when my great-grandfather passed away. I still remember going over to his apartment with my father

and brother and listening to his stories and jokes. Especially his jokes because no matter how many times he told them to me I always forgot the punch line. My great-grandfather was always the one who led our Passover Seders every year. After he died my many relatives stopped paying attention to the service that my grandfather now leads. My great-grandfather kept the spirit of Passover together and joined us all together in prayer, unfortunately he's not here anymore.

The name Abram can be a Biblical reference. The story of Genesis seems to chart the growth of Abram as he gets older and older.

A brown coat that produced a nickname: "Abram Brown." No matter how old you grow and how long you live, you cannot escape from death.

He appears to be the epitaph of entertainer. I imagine him as being similar to Mel Brooks, or maybe Dr. Seuss, as the words seem very lighthearted.

There is no mourning and no tears, no sweet memories or laughter. Almost gives me the impression that there is nothing beyond. The death did not disturb anyone. The feelings portrayed are neutral and non-committed.

This Abram Brown in the poem could be my neighbor or my brother. I have changed my mind. This is a really deep piece of literature. Wow!

It reminds me of poems I used to write when I was younger and I thought everything had to rhyme.

How close were the interpretations of the young people? The *Oxford Dictionary of Nursery Rhymes* says, "This nursery rhyme is a relic of a folk-play." We find in their answers all kinds of connections being made—to their lives, to the text and to the world. These students are on their way to becoming strong, independent readers. How can we help students activate this strategy of inferring, to notice how this complicated process works and how it will support their reading?

By designing an activity that encourages inferring, and then helping students to notice the process in action, you can demonstrate how to use this strategy in reading. You can choose a picture book to share with the class, and read it aloud, pausing as students reveal the inferences they are making. You may want to offer prompts, such as

- Why are the characters behaving in this way?
- What did the character really mean by what she said?
- What do you think might happen next?
- What is the author really saying?
- What does this story remind you of?
- What are the big ideas or themes in this text?

If you are working with a group or the whole class, ideas from one student will cause others to hitch-hike into the discussion. By recording these examples of inferring on a chart, the students can see how the thought process works, and how we must confirm, revise and alter our hypotheses as we read further along in the selection and, of course, as we talk about the text and hear other opinions.

Visualizing the Text

I grew up listening to radio dramas and comedies, where the airwaves delivered the images to my mind, aided by sound effects, the narrator and the actors. When we read, a similar process occurs, and we create pictures of what the print suggests, making movies in our heads. And these images are personal, each one of us building a visual world unlike any other. Reading words causes us to see pictures, which is understandable since words are only symbols, a code for capturing ideas and feelings.

Reflecting upon the meanings suggested by an artist's illustration can be an effective means of demonstrating visualization and the need to reconsider our thoughts as we learn more. For example, the cover of the novel such as *The Machinegunners* holds many puzzles that can be unraveled as the class works cooperatively to observe and to practice their inferencing abilities.

I photocopied the cover illustration and gave one copy to each group of five, asking them to figure out what is being portrayed by the artist. They were able to use the combined life connections of the members of the group in their struggle to make meanings from the visual signs in the picture. They noticed a great many details and, as they shared ideas, would exclaim, "Oh yeah, I see that now." One student who had lived in England suddenly made sense of the dummy in the wheelbarrow, shouting out, "It's a guy; it's Guy Fawkes Day!" We had to stop the talk while he informed the class of the conflict in England that resulted in the burning of an effigy, called a guy, on the fifth of November. It had taken almost half an hour to piece together all the inferences offered by the artist for those students to make sense of the cover illustration, and the vital piece of information was supplied from the experiential recesses of the one boy's mind, released by the energy of the brainstorming session.

The next logical step was to ask the students to consider what the book might be about, using only the information on the cover. The youngsters pieced together the basic plot outline of this complicated book, set so far outside the framework of their lives—Northern England during the Second World War, when a group of teenagers attempted to participate in the war effort by firing at enemy planes with a machine gun they had found in an enemy plane that had been shot down. It took very few prompts on my part to nudge them further into their inferencing, and they were now prepared to read the book.

Summarizing the Text

When I began teaching reading, I found the term *summarizing* in the manuals, and it usually related to the post-reading process of recounting in a few words what had happened in the text. It appeared to be a quick means of finding out what the young readers had thought about what they had read. I considered it similar to writing a précis. But, as a reading strategy that occurs during the act of reading as well as at the completion, it is valuable to share with students. Summarizing is an organizing and reorganizing strategy that allows us to categorize and classify the information we are gathering as readers, so that we can add it to our storehouse of knowledge and memory. We need to constantly connect the new information we garner from the text, and to find a way of making sense of it so that we can assimilate it into our ever-developing construct of knowledge. How would we ever remember the tons of data we receive as we read without systematically adding it or rejecting it in our schema of understanding?

We summarize constantly as we read, sorting out significant ideas and events and other bits and pieces of information. If we are reading a longer selection or a complex and difficult piece of writing, we need to pause and regroup every so often, coming to grips with a means of classifying the barrage of information we are receiving. We might make notes to help us connect and remember details so that we can focus on the big picture; we might check the table of contents to strengthen our awareness of where a section fits into the whole; we might reread the introduction to clarify the framework of the information we are meeting. What we do as effective readers is use the strategy of summarizing as we read, getting the gist of the text.

Irene Fountas and Gay Su Pinnell tell us in *Guiding Readers and Writers* that as teachers, we need to "help students to be able to abstract the important ideas and carry them forward as tools for thought." (p. 319)

✓ We can highlight the summarizing process by looking at various examples of concise writing, such as entries in a television guide, especially if the students have seen the show in question. By having them bring in a variety of these guides, you can select different summaries of the television show and ask the class to compare them: which is clearer; which contains more information; which represents the theme or intent of the show most clearly; how many words are used in each; what type of language is used (are the articles such as "a" or "the" omitted?).

✓ Writing summaries with partners or in small groups can effectively demonstrate this process to students. Photocopy a report from the newspaper and distribute copies to the groups, who then must summarize the article in twenty-five words or less. Their results can be shared with another group in an exchange, until an agreed-upon version is arrived at.

✓ Collect three or four reviews of a recent film and have the students examine them for examples of the reviewers summarizing events from the film, and for when the reviewers move into the processes of synthesizing and critiquing.

✓ The blurbs on the back covers of the novels the students are reading offer interesting examples of types of summaries, and can help the students to distinguish between information and opinion.

✓ Captions are useful examples of concise summaries. The students can create a collage of sports headlines and then discuss how headline writers have to summarize the events of the game, add personal comments, and attract readers, all in three or four words.

✓ Many textbooks offer summaries at the beginning and end of each section or chapter. Proficient readers know to make use of these cachements of ideas, both before reading and after completing the selection. When working with a text in a content area, it may be useful to spend time examining these reading aids directly, so that students can begin to add this strategy to their growing understanding of how we process lengthy or complicated text.

✓ During a literature group or in a conference, asking the students to begin the session by summarizing the events they have read so far can establish a supportive context for the next section, and help clear up misconceptions about what has happened previously.

Analyzing the Text

After English Class

I used to like "Stopping by Woods on a Snowy Evening"
I liked the coming darkness,
The jingle of the harness bells, breaking—and adding to—the stillness,
The gentle drift of snow…

But today the teacher told us what everything stood for:
The woods, the horse, the miles to go, the sleep—
They all have "hidden meanings."

It's grown so complicated that,
Next time I drive by,
I don't think I'll bother to stop.

Jean Little

Each of us has had in school the strangulating experience of analyzing a poem or a story to death, so by the end of the lesson we had lost whatever appreciation we had for the selection. Often the teacher felt this to be a necessary building block for future independent learning, but seldom did many of the students internalize the learning so that they could use it later.

Analysis and criticism are connected processes: before we give our opinions we need to carefully analyze the many aspects of the writer's craft that went into the creating of the work. We have all been disappointed by a student's review—"I hate this book" or "I love this book"—unsupported by any analysis of the points that resulted in the opinion.

We can help developing readers gain a deeper understanding of the text they are reading by giving them techniques for considering its effectiveness. As they learn to analyze the particular aspects of a selection, they may come to both appreciate the writer's craft and better understand their own responses to the text. They can begin to step back from the initial experience, to reflect more clearly about its effect on them and how the author conveyed the ideas and the emotions embedded in it. Our goal is not to dissect the selection but to notice how it works, how the author has built the text, whether we are reading an emotion-filled story or a resource containing information. We can help students discover the underlying organization, the elements that identify the genre, the format of the selection (including graphic support) and the overall effect of the work. For me, these are opportunities for guiding readers into a deeper awareness of the text, the author's techniques and their own developing responses. Critical reading relies on the readers employing all the strategies they know in order to come to thoughtful, carefully determined conclusions about the value of the author's work. As citizens, they will need to think critically about the life issues they will encounter, and analyzing texts with a questioning eye is part of the developing process.

✓ During guided reading sessions or during literature circles, we can help students move toward a critical interpretation of the text they are sharing. Analysis should be a component of every discussion, as students share their personal responses and connections, raise their concerns and questions, make inferences from the information and talk about different aspects of the content and the style. Readers can move toward a critical appreciation and understanding of the text, as the group members analyze and synthesize the ideas and responses that build cumulatively throughout the session. Each member should feel wiser about the text after the discussion.

✓ It is often helpful to engage the class in analytical discussions about a shared text, so that students can observe the strategy in action. Keeping a record of what is said on a chart or having students keep notes can support the reflective talk about the process. Using prompts such as these, we can guide their comments and questions about the text and the author's role in creating it:
— What type of selection is it?
— Does the text represent characteristics of the genre?
— What special language does the author use?
— Are the characters believable? Do they behave consistently?
— Is the author's background relevant to the selection?
— What new information do we find? Is it correct and complete?
— Are the themes connected to our lives?
— Is there bias or the use of unfounded opinions?
— Did the author engage your interest and maintain it?
— How does this text compare with similar ones you have read?
— Are you somehow better off for having read the selection?

✓ Contrasting and comparing can lead naturally to a more critical understanding of the content and the craft in a text. For example, students can read or listen to several versions of a story; they can chart similarities and differences in structure, style, content, language use, length of sentences and paragraphs and use of dialogue and narration. Then, they have some background and support when they comment on their choice. They have informed their opinions.

With a grade-six class in Manhattan, I read from the overhead screen Jane Yolen's short short story "The Promise."

The Promise

Deep in the forest she waited. Not even a stray wind broke the silence.

When she heard footsteps, she looked up, sighing deeply, not caring the hunters heard, her long wait over.

When the blanched, weary girl sat, the unicorn gratefully moved forward, putting her head into the promised lap.

Because its brevity surprised them, I read it aloud again to them. (It seems that many students wait to tune in until they think it is necessary; by then, this story is over.) We discussed the text in small groups and then shared our findings. The problem lay in connecting what they knew about unicorns with this truncated tale filled with incongruities. The students struggled to make sense of the ideas, examining every word and detail to try and build a larger picture that held together. They visualized, questioned, analyzed details, all in their attempts to find out what the story could mean to us who were reading it in that classroom. They used bits of information from films, cartoons, books, illustrations and history.

One student reexamined the title, wondering who had made the promise and to whom, when suddenly a boy blurted out, "What if the girl had promised the searchers? What if she was a decoy sent to trap the unicorn?" This caused much discussion and eventually most of the class accepted this point of view, supporting it with details from the story. But three hold-outs felt no maiden would betray a mythical beast, and felt certain the unicorn had promised to remain with the maiden.

These fifty minutes of thoughtful discussion were drawn from a fifty-word story. Most of the students were using their connections from life, from stories and from the text, to synthesize information about unicorns, hunters and maidens, and to construct for themselves a shocking new image of medieval archetypes, altering their unicorn worlds forever. And even the three hold-outs were comparing their versions of what might be with their classmates, and nervously and stubbornly hanging on.

Synthesizing Information from the Text

As we read, we continually glean new pieces of information from the text, often in a random fashion, which we then add to our personal knowledge in order to construct new understandings about the issues we are exploring. Piece by piece, we develop a more complete picture as new information merges with what we already know, and we begin to achieve new insights or change our perspective.

Stephanie Harvey and Anne Goudvis, in their helpful book *Strategies that Work*, say that "synthesizing involves putting together assorted parts to make a new whole." We synthesize the issues and ideas generated by our reading of the text in light of our own lives. When we synthesize, we change what we thought we knew; we expand our personal understanding. We move from recounting the new information into rethinking our own constructs of the world. We synthesize our new learning in order to consider the big ideas that affect our lives. We want to develop readers who construct meaning by summarizing the content and responding personally to what they have read, by reflecting on their process of reading and assimilating these aspects of learning into an holistic understanding of being literate.

✓ Retelling a story can assist students use the strategy of synthesizing to get to the significant issues. As they compare retellings, they can begin to notice the weight each teller places on different aspects of the story as they personalize their versions. We can list common themes found in the retellings on a chart, showing how we all struggle to move to the universal truths as we share narratives. It may help to have the students write a synthesis of the story they can then read aloud, and to have them find supportive information for their choices.

✓ Students are often plot victims; they simply recount the sequence of incidents that occurred in a story. The art of the teacher is to move them beyond synopsizing to a fuller consideration of what they have read and thought about. In the past, book reports were often simplistic recountings of plot: "and then he…" "and then she…" We want thoughtful, mindful interpretations and reflections of what they have read. We may be able to demonstrate a better strategy by having students use a double-column approach in their reading journals, for summarizing and synthesizing in writing. For example, they could work with the novel they have just finished reading: on the right, they summarize what happens in the story; on the left, they note their personal responses. The final written product can be a blending of the two columns. This separation and then integration of the two processes may help students notice the differences between summarizing and synthesizing. I use this parallel strategy with my graduate classes when they have difficulty knowing how to include their own voices and personal stories within their research papers. It takes several attempts before they feel secure enough to synthesize their readings with their lived experiences.

✓ After sharing a story, the students can generate questions stimulated by "I wonder…", questions that are not answered directly in the text but represent our thoughts about what might have happened. Looking at these questions, the students can examine the text for evidence that supports the prediction, clues left by the author that help us build a continuing picture of the characters or the events in the story. Using their background experiences and textual clues, they can examine their inferential techniques, noting when the discussion moves toward opinion, or when there is consensus on what might happen if the story were continued.

I was working with a grade-six class in a suburb of Toronto, where I read aloud the picture book *The Ghost Train* by Paul Yee, about a young girl whose father left China for Canada in the 1870s to work in the gold fields. When his letters stopped, his daughter made her way to the new land to attempt to find him. A gifted artist, she sold her paintings to pay her way, only to discover that her father had died in a mining accident. However, he returned to her in a dream and asked her to paint the ghost train that carried the lost souls of those who had died without proper burial in China, and to take the painting back home, burn it and bury the ashes that represented the remains of the lost workers. For the students, the tension of the story lay in the girl's having to destroy her creation, the painting of the train. They felt it was all she had left of the memory of her father's life after he had left her. Some were upset that she had obeyed his wishes; others felt she had no choice. We then gathered in two groups representing the two views, on either side of the room, and I asked each group to attempt to persuade each other to change their minds.

Their arguments revealed an unusual depth of thought, and a careful synthesis of every detail in the story:

> 1st student: By burning the painting, the dust of the remnants of the painting will filter through the very air the descendants will breathe, and those men who died will live on forever.

> 2nd student: The painting is only a representation of the dream she had in the New Land. Her returning to China with the story is the actual burial. The truth is now known, just as when the dog tags of the US soldiers were brought back from Viet Nam. That is the returning of the souls to the homeland.

> 3rd student: She should sell the painting. The mission is complete. The souls are at last home. The money she receives from the sale will sponsor her career. That will be the return of her father's true spirit, giving her the strength to build her life as an artist.

> 4th student: The train she saw was actually in her dream, and was telling her to go home, to return to China. It was her own soul she had to save. Dreams are just symbols; you have to interpret them.

In my own reading of the book, I had not thought of the episode as a dream. I know how this author fuses folklore and history, and I accepted this as a tale that he incorporated to illuminate the struggle of the immigrants. But the students led me in a different direction and opened up for me a new understanding of the book. This can only happen when we as teachers follow rather than lead the response to the text by those who were deeply involved. They listen to the story and observe the pictures, but they also experience the telling and the teller, and the force of the audience who is sharing in the experience. Why would they not have had a different experience from me? What we can do is discover with them what they think they saw and heard and felt, and help them to come to grips with their own and others' perceptions. I change as they change.

Interpreting and Appreciating Literature

Before I buy a ticket to a play, plan to see a film, or purchase a hardcover book, I do my research: I look for wise, informed critics who have read or seen the product, whose background as reviewers I know and trust, and who can represent their views and opinions artistically in their writing. I read the reviews in the weekend papers, *The New York Times* book section, the film reviews in *Maclean's* and the *New Yorker*, the lists of video and CD releases. I seldom pay attention to reviewers if I don't recognize them, if they reveal a lack of knowledge about their field or if I don't value the particular medium that handles their work. Criticism requires a particular stance, an analytical approach that involves a careful examination and consideration of the text, whether it is print or any other form of media. We search for informed opinion, ideas that can take us beyond our own limitations, that stretch us and enrich us, so we bring more depth of understanding to what we have experienced.

We want readers to carefully weigh evidence from a text in order to make a thoughtful decision regarding their own opinions, to combine textual information with their own background knowledge. They need to draw conclusions and apply logical thought to substantiate their interpretations. We want readers to make and to recognize informed opinions.

We want our students to work toward independence, to develop into life-long readers who see books as friendly objects, who recognize the art of reading, as Louise Rosenblatt, the authority on reader response, said, as the negotiation between the author and the reader. How can we help students think carefully about the texts they read, to become aware of how literature works?

As teachers, we can begin by providing students with a large quantity, a wide range and a great variety of experiences with the genre of story—all kinds of narratives, including fiction (fairy tales, folk tales, realistic fiction, novels, legends, mysteries, fantasy, adventure), nonfiction (diaries, biographies, encyclopedias, atlases, memoirs), poetry anthologies and picture books. Exposure to a wide range of books offers students the opportunity to learn how authors use language, since the language of literature differs from the language of daily conversations.

I long ago stopped thinking that there was a master list of what everyone should read, and moved towards supporting each reader's decisions about the print resources they selected—their newspaper, novels, magazines, work and organizational materials, and what they read for fun and satisfaction. As with films and television, appreciating literature is a developmental, life-long process, dependent on many variables—personal background, language and thinking processes, life experiences, familiarity with the type of selection, the purpose and payoff for reading, the situation in which the reading is taking place and especially the readers' attitudes toward texts, often determined by experiences in school. What I can do is open up the options that printed resources offer, and explore with readers how different texts work, what to look for and what to expect, so that they can be informed in the choices they will make and select the resources that give them the most satisfaction. Often that depends on the quality of the writing, whether it is the daily editorial or the gardening book they just purchased that spring.

How can we help our students interpret and appreciate the literature they will experience throughout their lives? We know that we read the same book through different eyes as we grow into our lives, and often we are shocked at our new response to a text we thought we knew with our hearts and minds. I reread *Black Beauty*, one of my favorite books from childhood, with a class of grade-six students, only to rediscover the tale of an anthropomorphic talking horse who represents the class structure of England a hundred years ago. I was now involved in reading a very different book from the one I had enjoyed some forty years before. Across time, my accumulated experiences from research and reading and relationships had altered my responses and reactions. My world of understanding had exploded. Similarly, students construct their meanings with a particular book from the viewpoint of their own developing experiences. We would not want them at twelve years of age to respond to a book in the same way a forty-year-old divorced teacher would. Who they are at this stage in life will determine to a great extent how they interact with a text.

As teachers, we have all experienced the disappointment that comes from a student revealing boredom or dissatisfaction with what we felt was a significant piece of literature. It is a complicated task finding appropriate and interesting books that represent quality literature for our students, but it is at the centre of our struggle to help them become appreciative readers who will always be "reading the word, reading the world." If only they would enjoy what we told them to enjoy, or like a book because we did. Backgrounds and abilities differ widely in the middle years, and we need to help young people begin to consider their responses to text, to reflect on why they feel as they do and to consider the author's role in determining how they responded to a selection of literature.

Preparing to Read

A student in Larry Swartz's fifth-grade class, after listening to what Larry thought was a helpful but extended pre-discussion of the issues about to be met in the story, called out, "Mr. Swartz, can we get on with it?"

We used to spend too much time preparing students for a reading selection, often much more time than they spent reading it: we pre-taught lists of unconnected words, wrote long blackboard notes about the author's life or presented our own outline of what the students were about to read. But there are occasions when we can help students to prepare for reading a particular text.

Tapping into Background Knowledge

Prior knowledge of the topic, previous exposure to the author's work or a personal connection to the theme—all these factors can increase a student's possibilities of making meaning with a particular text.

✓ Before students begin to read a text, such as a selection from a curriculum textbook, we can ask, "What do you already know about this topic?" By recording all their responses as the students brainstorm, we can then have them categorize or classify the information and identify what they want to find out. After reading, students then find a partner with whom they compare lists, and write questions they still need answered.

✓ We can sometimes increase their chances of success by providing some background knowledge that relates to the text by viewing films or listening to a story with a similar theme.

✓ If a group is about to undertake the reading of a text, we can help them conduct a more formal preview, including brainstorming questions based on information from the title and the cover, and predicting events that might occur based on this information. Questions can focus and extend the students' thinking about a particular aspect related to the material at hand. The discussion itself may also generate new questions and different predictions.

✓ When students continue reading a selection over several days, a brief review of material they have read may be necessary. We can help them tell the story to the point where the reading ended, write a short summary that they can read aloud, reread a passage in the text that summarizes recent events, or simply reread the last page that had been read. We can review aspects of the text, including chapter heads, supportive visual cues and vocabulary that the text contains. This is not to say that we pre-teach vocabulary, rather that we acquaint students with the type of terminology they are about to meet in their reading.

Noticing Text Features

One eighth-grade class examined tables of contents I had gathered from six different history textbooks. I wanted them to make connections about how the books appeared to be structured, why the information had been arranged in such a way and how the intent of each author team could be deduced from these opening pages. It became a literacy adventure, and we used the discoveries throughout the year with our own textbook as a guide for understanding how its authors attempted to make sense of history. The students were connecting their text with how other texts were designed and formatted. I wish they could have, as an informed class, chosen the course text that they had decided appeared most appropriate, but we did make use of the other five books they had examined in groups.

Students need to be immersed in books of all kinds in order to become proficient readers and writers. As well, they need to receive demonstrations of how books are constructed and used, since books vary in purpose, audience, format and organization, as well as in the publishing devices and designs they employ. Often classrooms with helpful reading and writing programs forget the difficulties inherent in using a single textbook for mathematics or science, or the complexities involved in reading information books from the library. The type of book may influence the language it uses and the way in which information is presented. This, in turn, will influence how the book will be read. Consider how dictionaries, novels, poetry anthologies, diaries and manuals differ. Some books can be read from beginning to end; others will require the reader to organize their reading in the following ways:

- scanning a book for a particular item of information
- referring to a glossary throughout the reading
- reading part or all of a book to better understand a concept
- reading part or all of a book to follow directions
- reading only a portion of a book

A Student Guide to Features of Nonfiction

We need to work with students to learn how to maximize time and effort when reading nonfiction. Helping them draw up a guideline such as the following example may help them to handle different types of texts:

- Notice the many different parts of a book: covers (back and front), copyright, preface, chapter headings, table of contents, epilogue, index, title page, dedication, glossary, spine, bibliography, appendix, endpapers.
- A basic knowledge of text layout can sometimes help you comprehend texts. A graphic outline or a diagram of information located in the text, can be used as a framework for note taking or summarizing information. Text organizers can signify a particular meaning: italics, captions, labels, illustrations and photographs, graphics, diagrams, maps, tables, charts, side bars, graphs, fonts and effects, titles, headings, use of color. Words can be enclosed in speech or thought balloons; some words may begin with capital letters, depending on their meaning or their position in a sentence; others may be highlighted through different graphic forms, be presented in lists, or be used as labels.
- Text structures, such as cause and effect, problem and solution, question and answer, comparison and contrast, description or sequence, are useful to note, since they help you see the organizational structure. Often special cue words such as "for example," and "in conclusion," or "how," "when," "where," "why" and "who" questions can point out the structure of the text.
- Take a quick look at the publication date. If the topic you're exploring is a current issue, an older book may be helpful in providing background information, but you'll need to find other sources of information.
- Look at the book's table of contents. Are the topics you're interested in included?
- Some nonfiction books contain a glossary. Sample some of the words and their definitions. Are both difficult to understand?
- A quick review of an index can tell you exactly what information the book contains.
- Not all information provided in a book will be useful. Look for chapter headings and subheadings that deal with information pertinent to your topic of study.
- Words and phrases like "they found," "finally" and "in conclusion" usually signify important statements. Watch for boxed information that may summarize important points in a section.

- As you skim the book, take a look at visuals such as illustrations, photographs, maps, charts, cross-sections, tables and boxed text, and sample some of them to determine their complexity.
- Sample a few paragraphs to determine the reading level. Do a quick check of paragraphs through the book. Can you understand the main point of each paragraph? Is the vocabulary comprehensible? Is the text printed at a comfortable size? Do the visuals and graphics support your reading, or present new information?
- Skimming and scanning can help you to read a piece quickly; e.g., check for missing information, check for conflicting information, confirm information.
- Review material gleaned from the book, then look at the questions you listed initially. How many questions were answered? Which questions remain unanswered? Did the book turn out to be a good source of information?

Monitoring Comprehension during Reading

How can we help students monitor their own reading comprehension? In the past, we would often introduce a text and be ready to follow up with activities, but we would leave the students to read the text independently. Traditionally, we assessed their reading after they finished reading, instead of helping them become aware of what is happening when meaning-making is interrupted or when they lose track or become confused. During the actual reading time, the content may be daunting, class noises may interfere with their reading, or the period of time may be too long for them to sustain concentration. Even proficient readers have times during reading when they find themselves lost or their mind wandering.

We all need strategies for repairing a breakdown in understanding while reading, otherwise we just plough on to the end of the selection, totally confused by what we are reading. Worse still is reading the text and waiting for someone to tell you about what you thought you had read. Instead, readers have to monitor their understanding and attempt to repair any breakdown in meaning-making. Students may need to improve fluency, adjust their reading rate, reread and, most importantly, increase their reading stamina through sustained engagement with text as they read intensively for a significant period of time. Often oral reading practice in a group results in little or no comprehension for limited or struggling readers, as they wait their turn and focus only on pronunciation. These students need to employ word-solving strategies as they read silently, and then interpret the words aloud.

Students need to be aware of these self-monitoring strategies as they read:

- Checking predictions and forming new ones
- Checking unanswered questions and forming new ones
- Checking comprehension by rereading
- Skimming and scanning to predict and confirm
- Linking prior knowledge to what they are reading

Identifying Words

It would be impossible to learn, one at a time, all the words we will meet in print. Therefore our brain classifies information about a word we meet in a text, working from the knowledge of word patterns built up from our experiences with print. We want to encourage students to use all the different strategies there are for recognizing and solving unknown words in their reading, long before they begin to read the selection aloud. We need to help students learn how to solve words while reading, not only before meeting the text or after the text has been completed.

We need to be careful of our requests to have students read orally if they don't have an opportunity to explore the text silently beforehand. In reading a text aloud, a student has to pronounce each word while demonstrating through the voice the meaning of the words being read. Unless it is a rehearsed reading, the student is unable to use a variety of strategies necessary for identifying unfamiliar or difficult words. To decode a word means to be able to say it and understand its meaning in the context of the whole text.

These strategies can help students deal with unfamiliar words:

Anticipating meaning
As readers, we expect text to make sense. When it doesn't, as for example, when we encounter difficult words, we need to use all the information we have to help us understand the word's meaning and pronunciation.

Word solving
When good readers come across a difficult word they may skip over it with a view to revisiting it later; they may predict a word's meaning based on context and check back by rereading the sentence; they may reread known words around the unknown word, look for roots and word endings as clues or locate sounds within the word. For example, sounding out a word—the usual strategy when a student is having difficulty—often relies on the reader's prior understanding of not each letter but the letter clusters in order to make meaning:

th-e in *the*

ph-one in *phone*

s-ch-ool in *school*

psy-cho-lo-gi-cal in *psychological*

We can demonstrate self-monitoring strategies in recognizing words that proficient readers use—thinking, predicting, sampling, confirming, self-correcting—by suggesting the following:

Does that word sound right?

Does it make sense in the story?

Skip the word and go on.

Does the word fit in the sentence?

Put in a word that makes sense.

Where have you seen that word before?

Do you know a word with the same sound in it?

Now what do you think it is?

Check the word with the picture.

Cross-checking print information

Good readers often check information gleaned from one cueing system against information from one or more systems (e.g., using the cue of the *-s* on *boys* against a picture of a group of boys, or the fact that the unknown word must be a noun). If the two sets of information are congruent, the reader can predict success.

Skimming and Scanning

Skimming and scanning are reading strategies students can use when reading for information, when rereading a text or when deciding whether to read a text. When we skim, we form a general picture of the text, and have a sense of the main ideas. When we scan a text, we have a specific goal in mind. We skim through a text looking for key words, focusing on headings and opening and end paragraphs.

- ✓ Working with computers offers constant opportunities for students in skimming and scanning, as they search, explore, select and scroll down.

- ✓ One way to introduce this strategy to students is to provide them with a text and a list of questions. Students then skim the text for answers within a set time limit.

✓ Playing games with phone books or dictionaries can demonstrate the need for quickly skimming text and scanning to find a name or a word.

Determining and Prioritizing Ideas

My own books are full of different-colored self-adhering stick-it notes; they hang out from the tops, bottoms and sides of almost every book on my shelves. Why haven't I made the teaching/learning connection and begun using these markers with students of all ages? As readers, we have to read the text, think about it and make conscious decisions about what we need to remember and learn. Sorting significant information from less important information means picking out the main ideas and noticing supporting details. Flagging text can help students begin the life-long process of learning to notice what is important in a text, to prioritize the information, sort through it for significance and mark in some way the points they will want to use or remember.

Traditionally, we have taught students that finding the main idea was the first step in understanding a text. Sometimes we meant a plot summary; other times we wanted to find a theme. Now we know that this is not a simple process, that there may be many ideas in a reading selection. What we need to do is assist young readers in learning how to determine what is important (especially in nonfiction material), what is necessary and relevant to the issues being discussed and what can be set aside.

Students may have been noting details and main ideas, writing them down in notebooks and highlighting them in their textbooks, but may still be unable to remember what it was they were trying to understand. For example, there is seldom any useful reason for finding the answers to a series of questions that ask students to locate or, even worse, to remember insignificant details from a novel. What we use in constructing meaning are the pieces of information that add to our growing understanding of what we want to find out or are ready to experience; these are details we can't do without, pieces of the puzzle necessary for creating the complete picture. The question has to be this: which details matter? In my own teaching, I try not to ask a student to locate a detail unless that piece of information is necessary for a deeper understanding of what is being explored. I want the student to search out the facts necessary for understanding, for supporting an idea or clarifying a point, not to rely on a treasure hunt for details that I determine to be important.

Marking and Highlighting Text

Anne Goudvis and Stephanie Harvey in *Strategies that Work* suggest organizing sessions with students where they explore various ways of marking text:

✓ Highlight markers are popular among older students. Unfortunately, these students have had little practice in recognizing what is important and often color in the entire page. They have had little or no instruction in sifting ideas. Conduct a demonstration in finding and selecting important ideas and supportive details by using copies of a common text and having the students compare their highlighted choices. Tovani and Harvey suggest having the students practice by using two colors of markers and highlighting every word: one color for what they understand and one color for puzzlements and confusions. In this way they can begin to distinguish what they know from what they don't understand. They can discuss possible strategies to clear up the difficulty.

✓ Distributing copies of a short text allows the students to mark or highlight the page, especially if the books normally used are school property. They can code on the copy what is happening as they read, noting questions and subsequent answers, connections they make as they read, inferences they determine, "aha" moments—making visible their own thinking patterns as they read. In partners or small groups, students can compare strategies, clarify difficulties and share insights.

✓ Colored stick-it notes can code prior experiences, thoughts, queries and reflections as we read, modeling a technique that many readers use in their reading lives. At the conclusion of the reading, these sticky markers can be pasted on a page so that the reading/thinking processes can be seen as a whole, and each student's pattern can be analyzed: Where were the difficulties? Which words or terms caused trouble? What questions arose? What connections were made? What was the author trying to say? How did I solve the confusion? What do I think about the topic now? Students can begin to see how they go about constructing meaning, identifying confusions and monitoring their own reading.

Self-Monitoring as Meaning-Makers

We need to help students stay on top of their reading, keeping track of how well they are understanding what they are reading, detecting obstacles and confusions that derail understanding, and understanding how to repair meaning when it breaks down. When something doesn't make sense or a problem arises in their understanding, experienced readers slow down, reread, clarify confusions, check for understanding and move to repair comprehension by accessing different strategies. Some readers simply lose track of meaning by "spacing out"; others see no purpose in what they are going to read; others have insufficient background knowledge to understand unfamiliar concepts or ideas, focus on details rather than on important ideas and information or maintain misconceptions as they read. They don't have enough strategies to select from when handling a variety of texts; they can't recognize the features of different genres or formats of texts in order to see the underlying framework that will help organize the concepts.

Readers need to overview the text, a form of skimming and scanning in order to determine important ideas and information while reading:

Activating prior knowledge

Noting characteristics of text such as length and structure, important headings and subheadings

Determining what to read and in what order

Determining what to pay attention to or ignore

Making notes in the margin

Highlighting necessary words and phrases

Noticing special cue words

Finding interesting or important information or facts

Noticing opinions

Finding larger themes

Deciding to quit the text or read it again carefully

Readers need to construct meaning as they go, repairing the meaning-making when it breaks down, going back and salvaging what they can, clarifying their thinking, noticing when they lose focus, rereading to enhance understanding, reading ahead to clarify meaning, questioning the text, disagreeing with information or logic, identifying and articulating what is confusing or puzzling about the text, drawing inferences, determining what is important and synthesizing their new learning.

Good readers read fluently: they use phrasing to communicate their meaning. When they read silently, they have the opportunity to interpret the text and add it to their knowledge base, giving them strength when they read orally. Less fluent readers, on the other hand, tend to read at the same speed—no matter what the text—both silently and orally, and to use the same phrasing. In repeated readings, a student practices reading one passage repeatedly until she or he can read it fluently (this will vary from student to student and depends on the degree of fluency, as well as accuracy). The benefits of repeated readings are numerous, particularly for at-risk readers, and carry over to other texts that they have not practiced, helping to increase fluency, word recognition and comprehension. Texts that lend themselves to this activity include picture books, poems and short stories. Choral speaking, script reading and preparing a story for sharing with reading buddies offer real reasons for rehearsing a text selection.

What, then, are some signs of reading breakdown that we can teach our students to notice and to rectify?

There are too many hard words in the selection, and I am giving up.

Generally speaking, if there are more than five difficult words on a page that the reader can't readily solve, the text is too difficult. Readers need to find an easier book or do some pre-work with the ideas, words or structure of the text. It seldom helps to look up a number of words in a dictionary before reading, but pre-teaching to recognize one or two important terms may help the reader understand other words in context. Often a discussion before reading can present the students with enough background and terminology to make meaning with the words. Of course, efficient readers know to omit a difficult word or to flag it until they have read further and have more information to bring to recognizing it.

I can't remember what I am reading about.

If a reader can't retell part of what has just been read, then he or she has to go back and take stock of the text, review the purpose for reading, do some more pre-work on the text or reread what has gone on before. There is little sense in continuing when they have lost their way. Readers need to stop and retell what they remember so far or consider what has happened previously in the story.

I don't care what I am reading about.

The reader has lost the purpose for reading the selection. There is no interaction with the author or the text. Instead of questioning the ideas on the page, arguing or wondering about the content, the reader has stopped interacting with the print. It might be helpful to have the student begin predicting what could happen next, and then rethink and revise their guesses as they find out more information.

I am thinking about something unconnected with the text.

All readers shift back and forth between the print and other ideas unrelated to the text. But the proficient reader recognizes this wandering, and attempts to connect with the ideas in the text by relating it to events in life. Guided reading sessions may help the reader to learn to stay on task.

I am not finding answers to the questions that I ask as I read the text.
The reader needs more background or clarification about the text before the meanings can build. If our questions begin to pile up as we read, we need to step back from the text and find a stronger orientation to what we are reading. Good readers learn to preview the text they are about to read, to notice its organizational structure, its format, how it fits in with their past reading and life experiences. In that sense, they need to read what they already know.

I can't create any visual images from the text.
If the reader can't make any pictures from the words in the text, then meaning has been interrupted, and the mind is not imagining what the words are creating. It takes practice to paint mental pictures from the text but, as the reader becomes more adept at visualizing, the ideas in the text grow clearer, and new connections can be made with the reader's background experiences.

I have read it but I have no idea what it was about.
By using some of the strategies they have explored during the year, students can become aware of their difficulties and work towards handling the confusion. Should they highlight information that puzzles them? Do they need to jot down questions that arise as they read? Should they reread the introduction or the blurb on the back cover? Do they need to check a difficult term in the glossary? Do they need a brief conference with the teacher to get them back on track? Can they begin to make connections with the text as they read, relating other background experiences, both in print and in life, to this text?

I am afraid to accept that I can't understand what I am reading.
By ignoring or disguising their confusion or a breakdown in their reading, or by not monitoring the problems they are having with meaning-making with a text, students can't make decisions about their comprehension problems and strengths. They can't find out how to bring themselves back to making sense with their reading. The first step may be to isolate the difficulty and select a strategy that can help. Sometimes writing down a response or a summary of what has been learned so far helps clarify the direction the text is taking. It may help to break the text into smaller pieces and discuss each text segment.

I never skim or scan to find main ideas or important facts; I never adjust my reading rate.
Often we need to scan the text to get the gist of it before we read the specific passage, or skim a page to find the point that connects to what we have just read. Readers need to understand the structure of text, to note any features that might help in understanding—captions, pictures, marginalia, summaries, etc.—and then bring that information back to their reading. As well, it often

helps to slow down the reading rate, to say a piece of dialogue aloud, to listen to the line of a poem as you speak the words. Similarly, you can read more quickly when the information is already familiar or a section is not useful.

Thinking Aloud

When we ask students to think aloud as they solve a reading difficulty, we can witness their thinking processes as they mark the text or jot down their ideas and questions. Articulating the process of how we think as we read helps students to become aware of the strategies they have on hand, and gives them strength as readers. When listening to students describing their thought processes, we need to refrain from asking leading questions, for they may assume that we are looking for a particular response. Instead, we can discuss how a particular strategy helps them to problem-solve. We can extend their learning by modeling aloud our own strategies in a think-aloud demonstration. Reading is a strategy-based activity; when students are aware of the strategies they need in order to read, they are more confident in their ability to tackle new text.

Responding to Text: Deepening and Extending Comprehension

Students need opportunities to deepen and expand their understanding of complex and multifaceted texts in deep and involving ways. When their reading experiences are extended and supported by their own written and artistic responses and those of their classmates, they can move into interpretation and appreciation, understanding the negotiation that is required in order to participate in the act of reading what others have written. They are learning to consider the complexities involved in the relationship of text and reader.

What we look for in responses to reading are instances where students

- challenge previous notions they had about a topic
- gain new learning through interacting with others
- discover a new way of viewing a character or an event
- see the story in a larger context
- check the accuracy of their predictions
- consider questions that were answered, and others that were unanswered
- review the main themes of the text
- think about what they have gained from reading and link it to their existing knowledge

- question, compare, evaluate and draw conclusions from their reading of the text
- reflect on the experience of the text and incorporate it into their lives
- represent their interpretations in a different mode, such as poetry

However, sometimes students spend more time on their responses to a text than on the act of reading. We need to encourage them in their reading, for it is the accumulation of positive, meaningful reading experiences that will drive them forward to become life-long readers. Through carefully designed response activities, we can nudge them into different and divergent levels of thinking, feeling and learning.

Keeping a Reading Journal

In reading journals, students can record their thoughts and feelings about the books they are reading, as well as keep a list of the books they have read. We often need to write about our thoughts before we can really come to grips with them. The act of revisiting and reconsidering our responses to a text is often possible by reviewing what we have written in our journals. In doing so, we are connecting the processes of reading and writing, formulating thoughtful and personal reactions to what we have read. By keeping a journal during the reading of the text, students can engage in a conversation with the author, record critical interpretations, monitor their own progress and record observations for later use in their writing projects or in a dialogue with the teacher. They may also include sketches or charts that support their responses. Ideally, they would write in their journals when ideas occur as they read, but it may be necessary to develop this as a technique by selecting a time in a guided session, or perhaps having them write an entry during every other reading occasion.

The Teacher's Response

Reading student journals allows you to have a literary conversation, often a private one, with each student several times throughout the year. Therefore it is extremely important that you read their journal entries as a truly interested and involved reader, and as an enabling teacher.

✓ Your written responses can guide your students towards a deeper consideration of what their reading has meant to them, as you reflect on their learning and the connections they seem to be making. The art of teaching lies in your comments: celebrating their insights, deepening their awareness and sharing your own connections to the texts of their lives.

✓ If you ask authentic questions and offer genuine comments and opinions, your message can connect with the student's in some way.

✓ By posing questions that involve rethinking or rereading on the part of the reader, you can help students consider what they have read in a different light or from another perspective. You can ask for more information or a clearer interpretation.

✓ You can recommend other authors or titles or genres, or books with similar themes or events.

✓ You can have an authentic conversation even if you haven't read the student's book, by valuing the student's responses and acknowledging his or her thoughts and feelings.

✓ You can model quality responses with your personal interactions.

✓ You can share your own experiences as a reader and writer, commenting on the authors and books you enjoy.

✓ You can come to know your students in more personal ways and learn more about them as readers and writers, and as people.

✓ You can gain important knowledge about their literacy abilities that can be used later as issues for mini-lessons and conferences.

✓ You can look for literacy growth, how the students are developing and refining their knowledge and opinions about reading; how they are discovering new authors and new genres and how they are gaining greater awareness of themselves as readers and writers.

✓ Some teachers write responses to five journals each day. Others have the students write them a letter once a week to summarize responses from their daily journal entries. In this type of letter, they can discuss what they have read or frame their reading experiences by synthesizing their thoughts. Occasionally, students can write back and forth to each other, having conversations about the different books they have read.

SUGGESTIONS FOR STUDENTS ON KEEPING READING JOURNALS

• make predictions about what may happen as the story progresses
• confirm your predictions, or refer to a previous entry you have made
• write about some surprises in the book, events and changes that you didn't anticipate or puzzles that concern you
• transcribe a memorable quote or a special bit of dialogue from the book
• turn a powerful piece of prose from the book into a found poem

---

- discuss the big ideas in the book, the issues that take you "from the words" and "into the world"
- discuss the genre of the book you are reading and be aware of the features of that particular type of writing
- discuss the cover illustration or other illustrations within the book, the layout of the book or its structure
- connect the book to other books you have read by this author, such as a prequel or a sequel
- write about a special character you are drawn to or feel connected to, or discuss the changes in the character as the story developed
- notice the author's craft and connect it to your own efforts at becoming a writer
- comment on the author's apparent purpose for writing the book
- notice the writer's language, the use of special words or expressions or memorable descriptions that stay with you
- comment on places in the book you have marked that in some way connect to your own life
- find connections to films and television programs, and to other books with similar themes
- give your own opinions about issues that have arisen from your reading the book
- examine the background and qualifications of the author
- question the accuracy of the author or challenge the author's ideas
- summarize the book or write a short précis about it
- discuss your difficulties and struggles as you read the book or your reason for abandoning it
- discuss what you have learned from reading this book

In Nancy Steele's class, reading journals are a vital part of the program. One student named Monica is an unusual, avid reader, and Nancy dialogues with her at different times throughout the year, sometimes trying to keep up with her.

Monica writes about *The Amber Spyglass* by Philip Pullman:

> A thrilling conclusion to Philip Pullman's Dark Materials trilogy, The Amber Spyglass follows The Golden Compass and The Subtle Knife both page turners and best sellers. The trilogy follows the life of Lyra and Will through many adventures in different worlds. Philip Pullman has an endless imagination, and the ability to create and bring to life hundreds of worlds and creatures. All three books are full of interesting philosophical ideas, based around the idea that there are millions of different worlds, all parallel to each other, each of them oblivious to the fact that they are not alone.
>
> Over the course of the trilogy, a celestial war unfolds when Lord Asriel tries to connect the worlds and create "The republic of

heaven." Each book has some sort of magical instrument in the centre of its plot — first, the Golden Compass, also known as the Aleitheometer. This aleitheometer can predict anything, it has the answers to everything. But it can only be read by a skilled few. Lyra is one of these — and the Golden Compass has a recurring role in all three books. The second is the Subtle Knife. Extremely powerful and dangerous, it can cut through anything as well as cut windows into other worlds. The third and final is the Amber Spyglass, which is created by the skilled scientist Marg Malone when she is in the world of the "muelfa" a strange wheeled creature. The Amber Spyglass can see "dust." Dust is at the centre of all three books. The church tries to destroy it, others worship it, without it people cannot exist.

But no one really knows what it is. Dust is tiny particles, not visible to the human eye. It is celestial material. It is sin, love, envy and life. At the end of reading the trilogy, I'm still not sure exactly what dust is.

These books are the best sci-fi-fantasy-mystery-thriller-philosophy books I have ever read! They're pretty long, and kind of hard to get through, but well worth it. Philip Pullman's other trilogy The Ruby in the Smoke, The Shadow of the North and The Tiger in the Well are amazing Victorian thrillers, full of dark mysteries and a sad love story. Just as good as His Dark Materials.

Her teacher, Nancy, writes back:

As you know we share many of the same favorite books so I am going to give the Pullman trilogy a try, as you loved it so. The sci-fi idea of parallel worlds has been developed by several writers. One of my favorites is Dianne Wynne Jones. I often recommend her to people who have loved the Harry Potter Series because she shares with J.K. Rowling the ability to create a very interesting and believable fantasy world. Have you read many of her books? Try The Lives of Christopher Chant.

Have you ever thought of the ethical component of these teen sci-fi/fantasy books? You mention that the 'dust' seems to have some relationship to good and evil but it is ambiguous. Do you think that Pullman is dealing with the theme of good and evil? So many sci-fi fantasy writers are. Madeleine L'Engle, whom I know you have read, has a very strong Judeo-Christian element in most of her books and most often the conflict involves destroying the agents of evil. I am fascinated that the church (Christian?) in the Pullman books is trying to destroy something that is necessary for existence. What do you think Pullman thinks about the church?

Talking about Texts

What seems to help readers in developing a deeper, more fully realized under-standing of a text is to share personal meanings and responses with others, par-ticipating in discussions with classmates in literature circles, book clubs or reading groups. By going public with their responses, readers increase the con-nections they can make with those who are reading alongside them, as individ-ual responses are both shared and altered by the contributions of the members and often by the nurturing support of the teacher.

We can frame literature journeys as inquiries, where students participate in the quest for increased understanding, making connections with what others are thinking out loud, as each member gropes and stumbles towards meaning. They surprise each other into knowing; they learn to hold their ideas tentative, to invite partners into the conversation, to enter the uncertain forest of ideas. It is the dynamic of the interplay among members of the literacy community that enables and engenders the processes of meaning-making. In school, our strength as educators lies in the interactions we establish among the students as they learn from and because of each other in socially constructed discourse.

Some students in Larry Swartz's class were engaged in text talk on their own, without any teacher intervention. However, they were used to this process of discussing in small groups as a normal part of the literacy program. Five sixth-grade students discussed their reactions, questions and predictions after having read silently the preface to the novel they were about to read, *The Music of the Dolphins* by Karen Hesse. The book begins with a reprint of a fictional newspaper article that reports the rescue of a wild young girl found swimming in the ocean between Cuba and Florida. Now a teenager, Mila has been raised by dolphins from the age of four.

T: Do you think she's a mermaid?

H: I'm not really sure.

N: I think she might be a real mermaid because she lives with dolphins and is in the water all the time.

S: ... or she might be brain-damaged or something.

T: Maybe she fell in the water when she was a little girl and everybody thinks she died.

H: But how would she breathe underwater and how would she live?

S: She'd breathe on top of the water and eats fish.

T: We need some more information about her.

N: I don't think the headline actually matches the newspaper article.

H: Actually, I do.

T: The headlines say that she's the wild child in the story.

N: I don't think they should actually call her 'wild'.

S: Maybe that's what they'd call you if you lived in the ocean most of your life.

N: For this story what do you think the whole book is going to be about? What problems will she have?

H: I think it's going to end up like a dream.

T: I think it's really happening.

S: I think the pilot just might be...

T: ... making it up.

S: Maybe they didn't have anything to talk about in the newspaper so they made it up.

T: Why would the newspaper write a story if it wasn't true? People must have seen her.

S: The girl just might have been swimming.

N: What I'm really wondering is where did she come from.

H: How did she get in the ocean?

T: Where did she find the dolphins?

S: She probably rides dolphins I think.

N: Maybe the dolphins are her only friends and her only way of survival.

H: Do you think she has a family?

N: She probably did...

T: It's like those stories that probably someone else brought her up...

H: ... Yeah...

T: She probably was in the water and saw the dolphins.

H: It's like the story of Tarzan.

T: She makes a high pitch cry like the gorilla.

H: This is Miami Florida. Some people think that there are mermaids in the water. You never know, he might just be seeing things or something.

S: I think a bunch of scientists are after this girl.

T: It says here (reading)...*This girl ran away, hiding in the mangroves.*

H: (reading) *She's between the age of eleven and sixteen years old.*

T: I think they should have put much more information in this article.

S: That's why we're having this conversation.

N: I have a feeling someone's going to find her and she's going to grow up with that person.

H: Someone's going to teach her all the things that she needs to know... teach her how to be a girl and send her to school, but then she doesn't like it.

S: I think they should put her back to the ocean. She's going to learn everything but it's not going to pay off.

H: She lived all her life in the ocean with dolphins. She can't change that fast.

N: Maybe she can only talk like dolphins. That's the only way she can communicate.

T: I think she communicates by singing. She sings to dolphins and they sing back to her.

H: I don't think men have the right to take her to the ocean. This is her habitat and this is where she lives.

T: This is her life.

H: Let her just live her life.

N: They just want to get rich...

H: ... by destroying somebody else's life.

Through their discussion, the group moved inside the text, making predictions ("I think a bunch of scientists are after this girl"), asking questions ("Do you think she has a family? Did she drown and come back to life?") and groping towards a sense of what they will be reading. As the students discussed the article, they seemed to be looking carefully at the author's words, making connections to stories that they knew ("It's like the story of Tarzan") and sharing concerns about survival and being abandoned ("I'd like to live with dolphins only part time but have a family that I could go to"). This type of group talk is concerned with exploring, speculating and arriving at understandings that no one child could have reached alone.

Encouraging Text Talk

In *Tell Me*, Aidan Chambers has provided a series of open-ended generic questions that can contribute to lively interchanges among students. Although the list in the book is extensive, he feels that the following four questions would stimulate discussion with students:

1. Tell me about the parts you liked the most.
2. Tell me about the parts you didn't like.
3. Was there anything that puzzled you?
4. Did you notice anything in the story or poem that made a pattern?

We can organize our talk time in a variety of ways:

✓ Students need time to reflect on a text and formulate their ideas before they discuss them with others. We can encourage them to record their responses to a text in their journals as a preparatory step to discussing them in peer and group situations. The act of recording a response may increase students' comfort level at later stages when sharing their ideas.

✓ Depending on the nature of the discussion, ideas stemming from small-group discussions can be shared among classmates. This form of sharing can be done by jigsaw grouping where each student, in his or her small group, takes a number from one to four. Students with the same number form a second group. New group members take turns sharing their previous group's discussion.

✓ In small groups, the students can meet on a regular basis to discuss books they have read. The book clubs could be organized according to various themes or genres: fiction, nonfiction, poetry, science fiction or mystery.

Telling and Retelling Stories

"Tell me what your reading is about" is still the most effective question we can ask after students have read a selection, either alone or with others. Retelling helps students activate their immediate recall of what they have heard. Each retelling will be unique. What is revealed in their retellings can give us important information about their understanding of the selection, how they internalized the content and what they remember as significant. They can, of course, write a brief summary or synopsis to use as a basis for oral retelling. When three or four students retell the same story one at a time, and if they are unable to hear each other's versions, they can then compare the different retellings, especially if the retellings have been sound recorded. It can be great fun to note the variations in word choice, style, tone, choice of narrator voice and plot line, as well as additions and omissions. This can be an exciting linguistic study for a group of young people.

Students like to listen to a well-told story—they see the stories in their minds and are free to interpret details based on their experiences. While storytelling can be an intimidating event for those of us who feel more comfortable holding a book, we need to experiment with the genre so that we can offer students another form of story. As well, students can tell stories they have listened to and read, participating in a variety of storytelling activities. My friend Bob Barton is a well-known international storyteller, and he is not fond of students being forced to tell stories publicly unless they volunteer and have other storying experiences to draw upon. The following activities acquaint students with the process of storytelling and can help them to explore the genre.

✓ The students sit in a circle on the floor so that they can all see each other. A subject or style of story is identified. A story is built as each student in turn contributes one (or two, or three, or more) words. A student may begin a new sentence at any appropriate moment. A student may add as much as he or she wishes to the story. A "talking stick" is held by each student when it is his or her turn to speak, and is passed on to the next student when the speaker stops (sometimes in mid-phrase). The teacher may stop and start speakers at random.

✓ Begin the activity by dividing the class into small groups and asking each person in a group to read the same story silently. When students have finished, number them off. On a pre-arranged signal, #1 from each group begins retelling until the signal sounds. Students #2 take over, then #3 and so on.

✓ Provide opportunities for students to prepare retellings of stories for younger students. The stories they retell should be at the younger students' interest and age level. Retellings could be incorporated as part of a buddy program or story circle time.

✓ After reading a story, students can retell it from various characters' points of view. One way this can be done is to have students form groups. Each group chooses or is assigned one character. Members work together to develop this character's retelling of the story. In turn, one member from each group retells the story from his or her point of view to the other groups.

Representing Responses Visually

Some students who experience difficulty writing their book responses or summarizing their reading may benefit from presenting their material through the use of a graphic organizer. Lucy Calkins reminds us to see this strategy as a way of making sense of the reading rather than an end in itself. It should be a rough draft of the reader's thinking and not a product to be mounted on the wall.

✓ Semantic maps can be used during pre-reading to record students' thoughts about what may be in the text, emerging from a brainstorming or discussion session. The activity focuses on activating prior knowledge and connecting to personal experiences. One way to build a semantic map is to write a word that represents the main idea of the text in the centre of a piece of paper, then write related categories in squares that are attached to the main word. Students then brainstorm details related to the categories.

✓ Plot organizers provide a visual means for organizing and analyzing events in a story. These organizers help students summarize a plot and understand its organization, and they act as models for students writing their own stories.

✓ A Venn diagram can represent comparisons and contrasting information within one story or book (e.g., settings) or between two or more books. It consists of two or more overlapping circles: the parts of the circles that do not intersect represent unique or contrasting attributes, while the intersecting sections depict shared or common characteristics that can be compared.

Representing ideas through art is not just for those who can't write fluently, and creating pictures is not just part of rehearsal for real writing. For readers of any age, images are part of the serious business of making meaning; they partner with words for communicating our inner designs. For example, what relationship exists between the visual and verbal in picture books? Could one stand without the other? Do they tell the same story? Students of all ages can draw and paint along with their writing and their responses to stories. Responding to a book through art frees students from worrying about their language abilities, a concern that many at-risk readers and ESL students share. A simple drawing of a poignant moment in the story speaks volumes about the student's reaction to a text. Art activities include

✓ constructing a visual time line or a story map

✓ illustrating what they believe is the most powerful moment in a story

✓ creating masks for dramatizations

✓ writing a personal picture book patterned after or suggested by the story

✓ filling their journals with their artwork, expressing their thinking, observations, ideas on assessments and revisions, description of process, future plans and reflections on their learning

✓ selecting words they met while reading a book. They can play with the words and their shapes, illustrating them, writing them in calligraphy, or creating three-dimensional effects.

✓ using drawing as an intermediary step between reading a text and discussion. They then share their sketches in small groups where other members can speculate on the artist's intent before listening to the interpretation.

Reading Orally

In today's classrooms, students and teachers read aloud throughout the day: stories and poems we've written; excerpts from other stories that we loved or wondered about; words that touch us or puzzle us; tales from before; stories about today and tomorrow; episodes from people's lives; poems that cry out for sounds in the air; letters from friends; stories about places where we have never wandered; stories about dogs and horses and mothers and granddads and eccentrics and students and school and city and countryside; stories of hope and death and wonder and fantasy. We read short stories and long stories and chapters that build up the tension for days. We read stories from album covers and music sheets, blurbs about writers from the backs of book jackets, titles, reviews and recommendations. As we read aloud, we fill the classroom with the voices of our ancestors, our friends, our authors, our poets, our documents, our native people, our researchers, our journalists, our ad writers. We story aloud.

Can we give students the strategies required by oral reading so that they will approach the process with interest and excitement, accepting the challenge of bringing someone else's words to life? This is perhaps the most complicated and sophisticated of all response modes. We need to carefully reexamine our motives and strategies for including oral reading in the language programs in our classrooms.

For students, the benefits of oral reading are numerous. It can improve their comprehension and enhance their interpretation skills. When used as a diagnostic tool, it allows us to assess pronunciation, fluency and reading strategies.

Oral reading should not be confused with round-robin reading, which involves one student reading, then another, and so on. This type of reading seldom improves reading or leads to a deeper understanding of print. Round-robin reading may even decrease a student's understanding and appreciation of the story. A student may decode beautifully yet understand little.

Oral reading of a selection can bring context and words to life if students have opportunities to prepare, practice and rehearse their reading. When they are comfortable with the text, they can participate in the sharing of it aloud. Whenever possible, we need to try to create situations that call for repeated readings of the same text; familiarity with a text can support a struggling reader's attempts to make more meaning, to acquire word knowledge or to read aloud successfully with a group. Regie Routman tells of a student who said that her first reading of the book was like a rough draft of her writing. I remember being in Larry Swartz's classroom years ago as they were preparing for a parents' night by chorally reading six poems by T.S. Eliot from his *Old Possum's Book of Practical Cats*, not the versions adapted for the musical, which the students had listened to as well and enjoyed. Their rambunctious and joyful interpretations of the complicated rhymes and unusual language still ring in my ears.

Teachers are usually surprised when I mention that teenagers prefer reading aloud to almost any other method of communication until I mention the tapes and CDs that they buy in the millions, expecting that the lyrics will be included inside the package so that they feel part of the music-making process. Many of us have forgotten the other literacies and how they connect to the literacy of print. Teachers who are not trained formally as musicians often express fear and uncertainty about engaging their students in music-learning activities. Sometimes that reticence can be lessened when music-making is compared to something more familiar, such as speaking and writing. Music has much in common with language. There is rhythm in music and language. There are accent, melody, tempo, dynamic, form and texture in both disciplines. And both have sophisticated symbol systems that require human expression and context for meaningful encoding.

My colleague Lee Willingham brings music to our faculty of education as he engages our student teachers in all kinds of music-making and learning—which by definition includes oral reading. He writes:

> There is nothing quite like the buzz you experience when your expressive voice, full of energy and resolve, *sings* a profoundly personal emotion from deep within. The act of music making that is engaged in the human spirit far surpasses the knowledge that one has in reading notation or mastering the theory, or the skill that one may have acquired in being able to reproduce a pitch exactly in tune. It is musical understanding.

Consider all the school events that can cause young people to breathe life into words in community read-aloud events:

✓ We can model purposeful oral reading by sharing enjoyable excerpts of a novel, by reading good stories each day, by reading poetry and plays and by encouraging students to read aloud only when there is a wanting and waiting audience—after an opportunity to rehearse, of course.

✓ They can join in with others as they read songs, verses and poems aloud from big books, individual copies or overhead transparencies and charts.

✓ They can work with a buddy from a younger class and delve deeply into the context of the story as they find ways to bring it to life. I am impressed with buddy programs that require the older students to have some training in how to assist their struggling reader and where they prepare for the session, debrief with the teacher and even keep a notebook chronicling their progress.

✓ They can read aloud sentences, phrases and words that are useful in proving a point during story discussion, responding with the words of others to support their own ideas.

✓ Readers theatre is a technique that allows the students to dramatize narration or selections from novels, short stories, folklore, picture books or poems, instead of reading aloud only scripted material. The students can have one person read the narration while others read the dialogue speeches, or they can explore who could read the different lines. For example, a character who speaks dialogue may also read the information in the narration that refers to him or her. Several students can read narration as a chorus. Little or no body movement is used in readers theatre. Instead, emphasis is placed on vocal performance.

✓ Assisted reading offers the student support during the reading of a text. After sharing the stories in *Toad and Frog* by Arnold Lobel, I enjoyed reading aloud the dialogue from the story with a student, where I read aloud one part and the student handled the other. Paired reading daily for ten minutes with an older reading buddy, another student, a volunteer or the teacher can often help a troubled reader. In echo reading, the experienced reader reads a line to be followed closely and then repeated by the student. Or the two partners read aloud and along together, and the student indicates when he or she can read alone. However, the reading partner joins in when help is needed with a difficult word or when the fluency falters. After, the tutor could note three or four of the words that were difficult for the student and record them on cards for practice during the next session.

✓ At the conclusion of a particular theme or unit, students can read interesting or significant findings, poems that touched them, excerpts that made connections, quotations from novels, personal writings from journals or writing folders that they feel will have special appeal for their class. The ritual of sharing and summarizing is vital to oral reading in many aspects of tribal life. We can incorporate this power into classroom teaching.

Selecting Appropriate Books

Imagine never being permitted to choose what you wanted to read. I think of my son who piled his books on his bed at bedtime, because he didn't know what he would select to read once he was under the covers. However, in high school, he was a victim of the one-book-a-year philosophy that pervades our school system. The one book was never written by a Canadian, a woman or a writer representing a minority. The books were usually chosen because they were available in the bookroom. Literature mustn't become a bitter pill youngsters must swallow only for the sake of the common culture.

In literacy teaching, the most significant life skill we can begin to develop in students is learning to choose reading resources that will be suitable for their needs and interests. The lives of young adolescents are full of friends, homework, sports, lessons and chores. At this stage, reading may find itself squeezed out of the timetable. However, school success is greatly determined by a student's literacy strengths, so we need to help young people find time for books, help them learn strategies for selecting them and, especially, support those readers who as yet are not fluent or independent. It is certainly not too late for these limited readers. Today's authors are providing books that are interesting enough to persuade them to continue reading, yet with a reading range that allows success. We need to be aware of books labeled "high interest/low vocabulary," since it is most often the search for meaning that drives a reader to continue reading and complete a book. Readability in a selection does not ensure success. For some students, the stories may have to be read to them or accompanied by tapes.

Nancy Steele found that her student Monica had, with her mother, kept a record of Monica's reading throughout her entire life at school. This document provides an amazing piece of research for those of us interested in how and why young people read, and what choices they make. Her selections represent the development of Monica's literacy and literary life and involve popular selections as well as books written by serious artists for young people (Tim Wynne-Jones, Cynthia Voigt, Rebecca Wells, Sue Townsend, Janet Lunn, Paula Danziger, J.K. Rowling, seven novels by Madeleine L'Engle, the dragon series by Anne McCaffrey) and for adults (Gerrald Durell, Fannie Flagg, Stuart McLean, Chaim Potok, Margaret Atwood).

Novels

I enjoy reading novels written for young adults as much as I do those written for adults. These authors seem to understand the needs of students, and there are many fine books from which to select. Novels for young adolescents allow readers to engage in a dialogue with an author on a wide range of topics at a deep emotional level. The themes of these novels reflect the development of young adolescents, their concern about their place in the adult world, ecology, peace, the future and the past.

Because of their well-developed reading abilities and mature interests, some adolescents may want to move into adult novels at this stage. However, many fine writers have written books especially for mature young readers; these sophisticated, sensitive works of art deserve a place in their lives. Such books provide opportunities for these readers to focus on issues that affect them at their own emotional level, but that also stretch their minds and imaginations and present them with complicated and interlocking structures for deep learning as well.

We read history in many different genres, and historical fiction can create a clear context for different times, places and people. Carefully researched, well written historical fiction can portray human experiences in realistic, engaging narratives that enable students to understand perspectives and ideas. Students learn to read like historians, constructing interpretations and reasoning through new ideas and information.

You can find recommendations for new and successful novels in professional journals, on web sites for schools and libraries, and from other teachers and students in your school. I was pleasantly surprised to find so many sites for authors of books for young adults on my computer, resources for keeping me up to date.

These authors represent a wide selection of writers who understand and value the needs and interests of students in the middle years, and who represent quality in this field of literature:

Grades 4–6

Lloyd Alexander	Jean Fritz	Francine Pascal
Avi	John Reynolds Gardiner	Katherine Paterson
Natalie Babbitt	Morris Gleitzman	Gary Paulsen
Judy Blume	Kevin Henkes	Robert Newton Peck
Betsy Byars	James Howe	J.K. Rowling
Matt Christopher	Dick King-Smith	Cynthia Rylant
Beverly Cleary	E.L. Konigsburg	Louis Sachar
Christopher Paul Curtis	Gordon Korman	Jon Scieszka
Roald Dahl	Gail Carson Levine	Donald Sobol
Paula Danziger	C.S. Lewis	Jerry Spinelli
Michael Dorris	Jean Little	William Steig
Cynthia de Felice	Lois Lowry	Eric Walters
Louise Fitzhugh	Anne M. Martin	Eric Wilson
Paul Fleischman	Lucy Maude Montgomery	Lawrence Yep
Ralph Fletcher	Phyllis Reynolds Naylor	
	Barbara Park	

Grades 7–9

David Almond
Avi
Francis Lia Block
Caroline Cooney
Susan Cooper
Robert Cormier
Sharon Creech
Karen Cushman
Paula Danziger
Brian Doyle
Lois Duncan
Anne Fine
Paula Fox
S.E. Hinton

Brian Jacques
Karen Hesse
Monica Hughes
M.E. Kerr
Madeleine L'Engle
Ursula LeGuin
Robert Lipsyte
Lois Lowry
Janet Lunn
Kevin Major
Anne McCaffrey
Farley Mowat
Walter Dean Myers
Kenneth Oppel
Katherine Paterson

Kit Pearson
Richard Peck
Rodman Philbrick
Philip Pullman
Gary Paulsen
Jerry Spinelli
Mildred Taylor
J.R.R. Tolkien
Sue Townsend
Cynthia Voigt
Eric Walters
Tim Wynne-Jones
Jane Yolen
Paul Zindel

Poetry

Reading three or four poetry anthologies in an evening is a pleasure for me, a chance to revisit the words and rhythms of childhood and to hone my ability to select those few poems that I know will reach this year's group of young people. And of course my collection of poems grows and grows. It has been a particular delight in my work to find each year student teachers who rediscover the pleasure that can be found from reading poems, and the enormous satisfaction that comes from sharing them with students. Each year for twenty-five years, students have come up to me and announced, "David, you must read this poet for children; he is great! His name is Shel Silverstein."

For youngsters in the middle years, poetry becomes a special category, emotionally condensed, meaningful moments of print that speak to them in ways that other genres can't. While few adults continue to read poetry, young people find it a special art form. If we model a great variety of poetry in our shared reading events and provide a wide selection of anthologies in our school and classroom libraries, students will often choose to read poems during independent reading times. I collect each new book by my favorite poets and anthologists for young people.

On the first morning of the school year in Larry Swartz's classroom, the students were greeted with a display of between 30 and 40 poetry anthologies, assembled from the permanent classroom collection, the school library and his own books. Larry invited each student to select an anthology to read during their first silent reading session, and explained that they were going to find some favorites as they browsed through the collection. His goal was to feature "a poem of the day" in the classroom, to share a variety of forms, a range of poets and a banquet of words, thoughts and images. Larry read the poems for the first two weeks but for the rest of the year the choices and the sharing would be the responsibility of his students. On the second day of school, the students each selected one poem that they felt they connected to and copied it on a large sheet of chart paper, which was later displayed in the room. They then had 28 poems of their choosing to share. Each day, one student was assigned to present his or her poem. These were later collected and placed in a classroom book.

In a cycle of four or five weeks, all the students presented and then the process was repeated. During each cycle, a focus was given for the sharing of the poems: rhyming poetry, concrete poetry, poems that have questions within, poems about the weather, animal poems, sports poems, poems that are 25 words or less or poems by a single poet.

On Friday afternoons they chose a favorite out of the five or more poems they had met over the week. "Education" by Eloise Greenfield, "Pizza Treatsa" by Douglas Florian, "The Uncertainty of the Poet" by Wendy Cope, "Famous" by Naomi Shihab Nye and "New Notebook" by Judith Thurman were some of their choices. In December and in March they reviewed the poems to select "the poem of the term." The winners were "The Dream Keeper" by Langston Hughes and "The Ice Cream Store" by Jack Prelutsky. "There Was Once a Whole World in the Scarecrow" by Brian Patten was the favorite poem of the year. Poetry lives among the choices of Larry's students.

The following list represents some of the poets and anthologists that I have found significant for students in the middle years:

Arnold Adoff	Robert Frost	Naomi Shihab Nye
James Berry	Nikki Giovanni	Brian Patten
Diane Dawber	Eloise Greenfield	Jack Prelutsky
David Day	Paul Janeczko	Michael Rosen
Emily Dickinson	Jean Little	Cynthia Rylant
Sheree Fitch	Myra Cohn Livingston	Shel Silverstein
Paul Fleischman	Roger McGough	James Stevenson
Douglas Florian	Judith Nicholls	

Nonfiction

In my own reading life, I read a great deal of nonfiction these days: biographies, professional books, health and diet books, magazines, cook books, two newspapers a day and, of course, computer screens. Traditionally, we didn't include many of these texts as literacy, and we excluded many readers from our reading community. Nowadays, I classify my reading genres differently: narrative, information and poetry. Even the health books I have read are full of anecdotes, stories to help readers understand the issues. Fortunately, in recent years, the quality of students' nonfiction books has risen dramatically, and many of these books have added to the world of literature.

Nonfiction resources shouldn't be something students wade through just to research an topic. Many nonfiction books available today offer significant literacy experiences because they represent some of our most important historical, geographical, scientific and artistic endeavors. Students are fascinated by many aspects of the world around them—the power and fury of volcanoes, the preservation of forests thousands of years old, the unearthing of ancient civilizations and the adventures of modern-day heroes. All quality writing is literature, and many nonfiction writers are artists—they bring to life events and situations so that readers can share a part of that experience. How we select nonfiction may differ from how we approach a novel. We need to share this information with our students as they begin to explore the nonfiction genre.

John Meyers, a specialist in global education, saves interesting articles concerning education in the widest sense from the newspapers he reads, copies them and shares them with his student teachers. This technique grows from his past work in secondary schools, where similar newspaper columns connected students to relevant world issues. These demonstrations would be carried out using five minutes of the class period, and his students read and discussed all kinds of concerns brought out by a variety of writers. As well, John is a regular contributor to editorial pages of several local and national dailies; he lives a literacy life. My own collection of articles snipped from the *New Yorker* magazine and *The New York Times* Sunday edition continues to grow. We need to share these brief contemporary essays and letters with our students, whenever we can. Reading also needs to be here and now, as well as there and then.

My colleague Kathy Broad recalled a time when she was working with Richie, a grade-seven student who experienced difficulties with reading comprehension and written expression, particularly in the content areas. As resource teacher, Kathy was assisting with his oral presentation assignment utilizing research resources. She realized that to engage Richie's interest and allow him to tap into his personal expertise, the project had to be based on his great passion—hockey. Richie struggled at school but was a tough and talented defenceman.

A trip to the school library for resources unearthed a slim volume about Bobby Hull. Kathy was surprised that Richie had selected that particular book, but realized it had to do with the longevity of Hull as a hockey legend as well as the heft—or lack thereof—of the reference book. After quickly perusing the book, Richie announced, "I'm not reading this whole thing!" In fact, time would not permit a thorough reading. Taking the opportunity to teach Richie how efficient readers make use of a table of contents, they read the chapter titles in order to determine which chapters would be most pertinent. As he read along, Richie came to one entitled "A Gentlemanly Player." This title stopped the hard-driving defenceman cold. What did that mean?

Kathy pointed out that reading the first paragraphs of that chapter might help clarify things. After skimming the first page, they learned that Hull was a constant target for checks by the other team and yet, despite his considerable size and strength, he very seldom retaliated. As they talked about "gentlemanly" play, Richie seemed puzzled. "You mean, he didn't hit back even when it was a 'cheapshotter'?" It was Kathy's turn to be confused. "What is a 'cheapshotter,' Rich?" she asked. Richie explained that cheapshotters gave "dirty hits" which hurt people. Through this discussion, Richie became fascinated with Bobby Hull.

His oral presentation turned out to be a very successful combination of his research and his current hockey knowledge. Richie may have learned to use the table of contents, but it was Kathy who learned the power of truly personal meaning-making and connections in the process of comprehension. Later, she discovered that Richie's interest in gentlemanly play was extremely relevant, for he was considered something of a cheapshotter himself.

Ian Hundey teaches history at our faculty, and his own love of reading is highlighted by his personal collection of books by John Buchan—he has more than 120. His teaching of history always begins with story. In *Canadian History*, one of his textbooks for adolescents, he describes the experiences of a four-teen-year-old British orphan who came to a Nova Scotia farm in the 1920s as one of thousands of Home Students—British orphans and students of poverty who were brought to Canada as farm laborers and domestics to start new lives. They had to work for their host family for a set term—often seven years—before they became independent.

> Well it was a lovely clean home and they fed me good but that's the most I can say for them because they had no heart whatsoever and didn't know what to expect of a boy of 14. I was very lonesome out there and he didn't help matters by dogging and ridiculing me constantly. He would ask me to get a whiffletree and I didn't know what he meant because I was from the city and as green as cabbage. Then he would go off the rocker and call me all sorts of names and I wasn't used to that. Once he threatened to horsewhip me for stumbling his horse, for he dearly loved his horses. Fall came and I can remember it as though it was yesterday for it was October 7, my birthday. It had snowed about six inches in the night and the apples hadn't been picked yet so he sent me into the orchard with a ladder to pick all the apples off the trees and be quick about it. I had on short pants and no mitts and it wasn't long before I was crying with the cold but I dared not leave. I swore then and there that if I ever got the opportunity I would run away. The

boss and his wife were going off to vote... . Just as soon as they got out of sight around the bend of the road I beat it for the house. I stuffed my things into a bag and wrote a short note: 'I'm going home, back to my mother, and if you try to bring me back I will burn down your barn. Goodbye.

The inclusion of this personal story brings students to a deeper understanding of the history of that particular time. Teachers working in different areas of the curriculum are now recognizing the significance of books that they can encourage their students not just to read, but to be affected and changed by. The world of nonfiction includes resources full of information and powerful writing by fine authors. We need to share these books with our students, to help them recognize and value the full spectrum of literacy.

The variety of nonfiction for students in the middle years is endless and depends on the curriculum areas you are exploring and the interests of your students. Consider using books such as *Ghost Liners: Exploring the World's Greatest Lost Ships* by Robert Ballard and Rick Archbold, Linda Granfield's *In Flanders Fields: The Story of the Poem by John McCrae*, Gary Paulsen's *My Life in Dog Years, Sharks* by Seymour Simon, and *Leonardo da Vinci* by Diane Stanley. The world of nonfiction as literature grows every day.

THREE

Writing Strategies

We have not always included all of the writing events that occur in the classroom as acts of written composition, which of course they are. We have at least replaced the inappropriate term *creative writing* with *writing*, but we still don't want to lose opportunities for exploring the different functions of writing. The British educator James Britton helped us classify writing under three broad functions—personal, informational and poetic writing. As well, genre theorists have demonstrated that different functions for writing demand different ways of writing and of reading: a research report and a poem are two different linguistic and literacy events.

Each writing function requires different strategies, and we need to help our students become aware of them. However, we do know that students write best about issues and topics that matter to them.

It may help to classify writing events with your students in three categories:

1. **independent writing projects**, regular opportunities for students to work independently on topics they usually select for themselves
2. **research inquiry** drawn from the curriculum, although at times we may assign the topic from a theme or genre we are exploring as a community
3. **guided writing instruction**, with a group of writers gathered together temporarily to work on target areas of writing techniques and strategies, such as conventions, genre study or technological help

Much of our writing is personal, meant for only our eyes. We seldom edit this writing. Other writing events are meant to be communicated, and these we need to consider again. An open and accepting writing environment in our classrooms will offer a range of writing experiences and products, including diaries, journals, letters, surveys, how-to books, games, résumés, bibliographies, autobiographies, lyrics, poems, articles, editorials, essays, memos, advertisements, commercials, brochures, questionnaires, petitions, dialogues, screenplays and legends.

Generating Ideas for Independent Writing

"What will I write about?" Students have asked this question for generations. The first significant set of strategies we need to focus on should involve helping them create a horde of ideas that they care about, topics that call for their personal responses. For years, I thought that it was my job to provide those topics, but now I know that my role is to work with my students in negotiating what is significant in their lives. In their independent writing projects, students will need to choose a topic that matters to them. Since they will be working for an extended length of time composing and revising, and perhaps publishing, what they are writing about becomes paramount. Students need to explore their interests as they hone in on topics, probing issues, deciding on the genre and format, the style and audience, and referring to the models they have experienced in their reading and in their life connections. Determining which ideas should be developed further is an important decision to make before beginning the writing process.

✓ We can support students by encouraging them to record ideas and observations in their writing notebooks for future use. Some will select writings from their notebooks to use as inspiration for a longer piece.

✓ During brainstorming sessions on a particular issue, students can write down all of their ideas so they have something concrete to consider developing into a writing project.

✓ When students demonstrate an interest in a particular aspect of a curriculum area, that may be the stimulus for an extended writing research project.

Keeping a Writer's Notebook

Writing notebooks can become valuable resources for young writers. They can capture the seeds of ideas to be developed later as independent writing projects, jotting down images or events, recording memorable words, phrases, or what Bill Moore calls "Short Bits"—snippets of conversation, a line from an advertisement, an example of rich language use—sketching artifacts that may be significant, or gluing poems and documents that hold further interest. These entries may be a random means of practicing how writers work. One of my favorite educators on writing, Ralph Fletcher, in his book *What a Writer Needs*, says we need a place to record "our thoughts, feelings, sensations, and opinions or they will pass through us like the air we breathe." Young writers need to explore, experiment, look inward, discover what matters, and as Nancie Atwell writes in *In the Middle*, "name and examine their thoughts and feelings." In writing notebooks, students can write about things that matter in interesting ways, clarify their personal concerns and explore social issues. I wish that I had kept a writing notebook while I was growing up.

During our mini-lessons, we can open up the possibilities for the records and observations that can be kept in a notebook. It is most helpful if the class brainstorms a list of possible entries, adding to their own list throughout the year. These suggestions might help them get started:

- writing about special events at home
- noting the unusual behaviors of your pets
- sketching observations of happenings at school and at home
- gluing in a special poem or a letter
- remembering moments from a holiday or camp
- listing books and films you have enjoyed
- remembering characters and incidents in books you have read
- writing down memorable quotations
- including photos of friends and family
- retelling family stories
- freezing a moment in time
- keeping an idea for a story
- creating a web of ideas about an interesting issue
- getting something off your mind
- working through problems
- naming your worries
- recording your hopes and dreams

Natasha's Notebook

November 7
Dear Minnie,
I love writing on a nice clean page in my notebook. It smells like cookies fresh from the oven. I like writing on that clean page about the day and my secrets. Then when you're done your whole notebook, you can save all your great memories till you're a mom or a grandmother, and you could tell your children, "That's what I was like when I wrote in my notebook."

Writing in her notebook was a significant daily ritual for Natasha. On the first day of school in Larry Swartz's class, each of the students was given a hardbound, brightly colored notebook to begin their journey as writers. On September 3, Natasha named her magenta notebook *Minnie* and wrote about what she did on her summer vacation. On the dedication page, she wrote *WARNING! Nobody under the age of 208 can read this.*

In the next few days Natasha wrote about a breakfast her mom had made, a response to the picture book *The Relatives Came* by Cynthia Rylant, and a visit to her uncle. Her next entry was written while riding in the family car because Natasha thought that driving "would give me good ideas." After one week, Natasha was starting to need her notebook by her side at all times.

Natasha's journal helped her observe and reflect upon her world. She wrote mostly about topics of her own choosing, and experimented with a complete spectrum of genres: a description of a wedding she attended; an argument she had with her sister; a game she played at recess; a favorite sentence from a book she had read ("The colors of my father's dreams faded without a sigh"); the instructions to a string design she made; a tomato-picking outing with her family; a visit to the library; a poem about the darkness of the night; a visit from her Aunt; taking a warm bath when she was feeling sick; receiving a gift of labels from her mother; a story in three parts about a girl named Bloody Mary; a description of a mask that was displayed in her family's living room; a funeral; a math lesson about surveys; a meeting with her teacher; an interview with an imaginary friend; a joke (What is the best thing you can give parents on the holidays?/A list of everything you want); a retelling of a ghost story by Alvin Schwartz; a description of getting her school picture taken and many entries about writing in her notebook ("People take newspapers in the bathroom but I'm taking my notebook because I won't get bored").

Natasha's notebook is festooned with many drawings, stickers, captions, stick-it notes, cartoons and souvenirs. She glued down a nickel showing the face of the queen with the caption "This is Princess Diana's mother-in-law," traced her hand, made a border of colored hearts around an entry about a friend, inserted a math quiz she did well on, cut out and glued in a map of Africa "because my mother comes from Africa," brainstormed a list of words that begin with *ch-*, drew and labeled twenty bottles of her nail polish colors, saved a score sheet from a board game, included a survey of her classmates' favorite picture book they read that week, made a comic-book story about two friends, added a dozen animal stickers to a page and wrote a dialogue balloon for each one, transcribed a line of poetry that she discovered, drew a map to her house from the school and, after reading a James Stevenson picture book, made a comparison chart of things that are "Fun" and things that are "No Fun." On one page, a thin strip of paper had been rolled up into a scroll and glued on the page; when the piece of paper was opened, you could read Natasha's words: "This is my sister's blabbing tongue. It goes on and on and on and on."

Natasha personified Minnie and would often ask "her" questions and share "her" feelings—("I am going to give you a crossword puzzle to solve." "Don't you think it would be cool if everybody could be perfect?" "How did you feel when you were in the store and Mr. Swartz bought you for me?" "Are you going to cry when I write on the last page?") As Natasha was coming to the end of her notebook, she regretted having to say goodbye to Minnie, but wrote that she couldn't wait to write in a new one. She asked Minnie for advice on what to call her next notebook—"Do you like the name Jill?"

Natasha went on to fill seven notebooks of different sizes that year. She was intrigued with Ralph Fletcher's framework for writing notebooks, which had been outlined in class. She often used the notebooks of her classmates and teachers as models for writing, and they used hers for theirs. She blends diary and journal writing, and while some teachers see journal writing as a more focused writing tool, it is a joy to read this young girl's entries. Natasha is certainly a writer.

Natasha is fortunate that her teacher organized and encouraged her to write down her life. I wished I could begin my career in teaching all over again when I read Mary Rose O'Reilley's book *Radical Presence: Teaching as Contemplative Practice*. She presents her process for drawing her class to a close: "Write a moment and gather your thoughts on today's discussion; come to some experience of closure." Then, after fifteen minutes, she asks: "Does anyone wish to speak out of the silence? Share any final thoughts?" And time and time again, students thank each other, and the room fills with respect because of this gentle closing. She reminds us that school may be a sacred space for many students, perhaps the only site of reflection in their multimedia-filled culture.

Revising the Writing

Like most writers, my own work is cyclical: I write, revise, read, write, edit, read, write, think, dream and begin again. Students need to realize that writing by definition is recursive: we consider ideas, revise, find more information, edit what we have written, count how many words we have typed, share our draft writings, find a published model that interests us, reorganize what we have so far and sometimes give up and start on another project.

Through rereading the writing, by reading the work out loud but privately, by conferencing with peers and with the teacher, students can see changes they want and need to make in their writing as they refine their first drafts. We need to help students understand that revising and editing are important and essential processes to undertake when preparing a piece of writing for publication. Many students realize the need for editing, but have difficulty revising their ideas and changing the structure of their writing. When examining early drafts, then, we need to look beyond spelling and grammar errors in our initial conversations with young writers.

As a young teacher, I didn't know the elements of the writer's craft, and I didn't know how to help my students develop their writing. As I began to read fine books written for young people, to take education courses and to read professional books, I began to understand how writers work and what goes into making our writing stronger. But it was when I began to write myself that I recognized the struggle writers go through to move ideas from the head to the page so that others can have some hope of understanding what they are attempting to say. Before, I thought I knew what it was I wanted to say. Now my thoughts grow because I write.

Learning the Writer's Craft

During a visit to our faculty by the British poet Gareth Owen, he was asked a question about improving students' writing. One simple suggestion he offered was to place prompts around the room that could act as support cues for young writers. He mentioned that, after demonstrating a list of clausal conjunctions with his class, their writing structures altered almost immediately. Lately, Ralph Fletcher has helped us all look more carefully at the elements of writing, and we now know a variety of strategies that we can open up to our students:

- finding the appropriate voice
- selecting a genre that supports the purpose for writing
- reviewing favorite books to note the authors' techniques
- using a variety of sentence types that flow well, combining them where possible, and eliminating sentence fragments
- clarifying ideas that are vague
- adding important details
- showing rather than telling, by describing action and events
- sequencing ideas and eliminating repetition or unnecessary ideas or information
- incorporating natural-sounding dialogue
- choosing a powerful lead
- having a strong conclusion
- describing the setting
- giving necessary background
- developing a character fully
- using flashbacks and flash forwards
- creating careful transitions in time and place to help the flow of the writing

- choosing an effective title
- including all necessary information
- excluding sections that are repetitive or that stray from the topic
- ordering the information logically
- making good word choices—precise nouns, strong verbs, effective adjectives and adverbs—not always the first word that flows from your pen
- replacing overused words like "nice," "said," "a lot," and words you have repeated
- looking up synonyms for a word in a thesaurus, and using an unusual word you have discovered
- finding a rhyming word in a rhyming dictionary
- using an effective metaphor or simile

We now know that there are many things to teach about writing through mini-lessons, demonstrations or conferences. As well, students can brainstorm a list of craft items and add to it throughout the year. But I know that for me, acquiring the bits and pieces of the writer's craft requires as much time as it takes the cabinetmaker to learn how to handle different kinds of wood; mentoring, mistakes and reflection will be part of the learning. We can only help our young writers with what they can achieve at this moment in their writing lives.

Editing the Writing

We need to make students aware that what most interests us about their writing is what they have to say, not just their errors. Students may be motivated to refine and polish their work when they are preparing it for an authentic audience. To assist them, we can have a variety of writing resources available in the classroom: dictionaries, thesauruses, computer centres, word games and quotations by famous authors and poets. Writers often benefit from leaving their writing for a day or two. A fresh reading often highlights necessary changes. All students need to see themselves as writers. Sharing a published piece by each student in the classroom at various points in the year is a positive reinforcement for their work.

✓ As a demonstration, you can select a piece of draft writing that needs revising from a student's portfolio from a previous year, or create a piece of writing that demonstrates the specific editing issues you want the students to examine. Transcribe it onto a transparency or make individual copies. Then, in small groups, the students can read the piece as editors and indicate where revision is needed. To model the editing process, incorporate their suggestions by crossing out, adding and deleting information.

✓ It often helps if you monitor your students' work, and look for an example that documents the various stages of the editing process. With the author's permission, you can display his or her drafts to illustrate the revision process to others. Students can then examine the drafts and use them as models for their own writing.

✓ If you share your own draft writing with the students, they can make suggestions for improvement. Having the chance to see you—the teacher—revising your writing helps them understand the reasons we all have for revision.

✓ After selecting a well written, short nonfiction text of four or five paragraphs, you can mix the paragraphs before giving them to a pair of students to place in order. This activity helps them to read for meaning, and reinforces the concept that paragraphs contain discrete chunks of information that relate to one topic. When they are finished, students can compare their work with the original text.

✓ You can select a text that is approximately one page long, then retype the text and run the paragraphs together. The students in small groups can decide where the paragraphs should be separated, cut the text apart to create paragraphs and then tape them together. When they are finished, groups can share and compare their work.

✓ We can encourage students to reflect on their writing in their notebooks, noting problems they have solved, and things they have to work on. Students can write briefly about strategies they have used to grow as writers.

Publishing the Writing

The computer has changed our school publishing projects forever in so many ways. However, there is still room for handwriting certain types of writing (e.g., thank-you notes), for personal illustrations and for the art of calligraphy. I enjoy seeing student work carried to the publishing stage, for it provides purpose for the students' writing and a valid reason for revising and editing. Each student can publish or display one piece of writing each month, and they can share their writing on networks of young writers on the Internet. Young writers can enhance their work through fonts, color, spreadsheets, graphs and photos, and they can make books in dozens of formats:

diaries	photographs	miniature books
albums	wordless books	scrolls
recipe books	brochures	alphabet books
comic strips	question & answer books	scripts
re-illustrated books	shape books	timelines
instructions	letters and envelopes	

Reading their Words Aloud

David was twelve years old. An intense, bright student, he worried about everything. Poetry seemed to give him a vehicle for expressing his own fears. His writings were brief but condensed. In our sharing time, I often enjoyed reading the writings of the students aloud, but in this case, I made a serious error: I read it carefully as it had been edited but, as I finished, David left the room. I followed him into the hall, and he said; "You read my poem wrong. You said *stars* and I wrote *stares*." This editing problem had caused him pain, and I apologized, brought him back in, and read the poem again. I never took my students' work for granted after that, and now conferences have changed how I work with young writers, and how I read their writings.

Alone

On a window sill
three feet by one
Five stories up
The window is locked
People stare, laugh
But none try to help.
Different, very different,
Not like people at all.
I know their habits.
I watch always.
Their stares never cease.

David

Selecting Patterns for Writing

I have in the last year found several books for middle-year readers about basketball: *The Basket Counts* by Arnold Adoff, *Slam Dunk* by Lillian Morrison, *Swish* by Bill Martin Jr. and *Tall Tales* by Charles R. Smith Jr. It took a long time for writers to match the particular interests of so many of our students. But what strikes me is the unusual format of each book: it's as if the printer went wild and filled the page with words and phrases that twist and turn, jump and rebound, bounce and loop. The visuals are similar—collages and bits and pieces that move the eye all over the page. Thirty years ago, Bill Martin's readers, *The Sounds of Language*, did exactly this, and it has taken us a long time to catch up. With computer screens offering imaged print shapes at the touch of a mouse, students are familiar with using fonts and different text shapes, but schools plough on with very traditional forms of text. What if we provided students with opportunities to experiment with a variety of formats that could be useful in shaping what they have to say? They can try to shape their thoughts and feelings with different genres, formats or graphic layouts. Often a visual pattern will suddenly open up writing pathways for young writers. We spend a great deal of our time exploring picture books with them, and they spend most of their time with comic books, magazines and computer images, and yet so much of their composing work is bereft of any visual contribution.

As this book attests, I have worked a great deal with Larry Swartz's class of students and, in gratitude, I wrote them a small poem and mailed it to them.

Sad Thoughts of What Must Be

Somewhere
in the woods
Stands a tree
near the stream
Stares an owl
in the night
Shines the moon
on the rise
Sits a mouse
near his hole
Soars the feathers
on the wings
Strikes the victim
of the night
Sings the cycle
of the world
Set inside
the silent woods.

True to his truly professional nature as a teacher, Larry used that experience as a resource for more and more writing. I received a booklet of poems the students had written, all patterned after the shape of mine, and all connected to the theme of our impressions of nature. And yet the formats of their poems somehow freed them to use words in different ways, to structure the lines in unusual ways, and to explore how they could mold their ideas into new shapes, which would in turn alter their messages. We have, in teaching, underestimated the power of patterns for capturing thought.

The Owl and The Mouse

I am the owl
Sleeping in the day
howling in the night
I am the owl.
I am the mouse
hunting in the day
dying in the night
I am the mouse.

                Jeffrey

Tiger

I am the Tiger.
I am stripes streaking
I am sun running
I am the Tiger
Cousin of Lion
Brother of Panther
Father of Lynx
I am the Tiger.

                Sara

The Owl Strikes Tonight

I am
Owl
hungry
for a
mouse.
I wait
for victims
to creep
slowly
beneath me.
In a flash
I'll dive
down to
scoop up
my victims
and fly
back to
my home
to feed
my hungry owlets.

                Chris

Genres, formats and shapes offer us supportive structures for writing down our thoughts and feelings. We hitch-hike along with the writers and artists who have motivated us into action, taking off from their initial creations but making the work our own. We can transform a selection of print into another mode, take the essence of the text and rework it into another form, such as rethinking an excerpt from a novel as a poem. This often necessitates shifting the point of view, and may lead to a deeper understanding of the text that is being patterned.

Retelling is another way of transforming print. Both oral and written retellings permit students to reveal their ideas about what the story means to them, encouraging imaginative and personalized recreations of the original.

Patterns and shapes for writing can present creative frames that help us to order or arrange our ideas. We can write

alphabet books	scripts	graffiti
chants	posters	horoscopes
fables	notices	applications
greeting cards	yarns	memos
haiku	advertisements	novels
interviews	brochures	questionnaires
legends	detective stories	yearbooks

Writing in Different Genres

We now use the term *genre* to classify texts by particular characteristics determined by function: to inform, to give opinions, to instruct, to report, to recollect, to tell a story. Traditionally, we talked about fiction and nonfiction, but we have all encountered texts that share multiple characteristics. Many novelists include historical or local information in the setting, the plot or even the characters. My aunt has just finished reading a novel set in Sarnia, Ontario, where she herself lives, and led quite a lively discussion on the places mentioned, even asking her niece if she knew the author—which she did, and provided information that challenged the blurb on the back of the book. Similarly, books of information are often written in the first person, such as the medical accounts by Oliver Sachs in *The Man Who Mistook His Wife for a Hat*.

Writing Letters

One of the simplest things for youngsters to write is a letter to someone they know. Unfortunately, in my first year of teaching, my students, to a person, wrote letters to John Smith, someone they had never heard of or had no reason to write to. He was created by the author of the textbook we had used as a reason for learning about the friendly letter, and dutifully we all wrote to no one we knew about nothing we cared about. Not only that: we wrote those letters "in rough" and then "in good." And we wrote the good drafts with straight pen and ink. At the same time, I had a student in the hospital with leukemia; no one wrote to him. Out of this act of thoughtlessness grew my struggle for creating for my students authentic reasons for reading and writing in my classroom.

Today we have books of letters that we read, written from everyone from soldiers in war to figures from history. I don't know anyone who isn't happy to receive a letter from someone they care about; we even tie some of them with a ribbon and save them for the rest of our lives. I would like our classrooms filled with the writing and receiving of letters, notes, cards, memos and, of course, e-mail. I answer 30 to 40 electronic letters a day; some I craft carefully, some are conversational. It is such a functional way of keeping in touch with my students and friends. I met an eighth-grade teacher who e-mails each of her students once a week, and those students write back. But for me, as useful as they are, these flashes of onscreen print are not a replacement for opening the envelope and seeing a human life ensconced in the shaping of those letter shapes. I shall keep my son's letters to me, in a small carved box, forever.

I find it so strange that we in school have minimized the learning and the human contact found in writing and reading letters, to the point where what seemed to matter to us were terms such as "salutation" (which no one ever uses in their lives). There is so much to learn about writing different types of letters. What better motivation for our students for putting down their thoughts for someone else to read? Why not have a "real letter week" and collect, display and read with the students all kinds and types of letters, perhaps in different languages, and talk about all of the linguistic functions that are evident in them? Twelve-year-old Peter wrote and rewrote this letter out of frustration and despair: maybe it helped. He was the victim of bullying, and he wrote to the parents of the accused child, giving his viewpoint of the incidents that had occurred at school. The letter was written after a series of meetings with the two students involved, and as the behavior continued. Many anti-bullying programs are using similar strategies. Writing our feelings down sometimes helps distance the problem.

Dear Mr. and Mrs. Lawrence:

This letter concerns your son Justin's behavior and attitude towards me. I am enjoying High School very much, but my feelings and work habits are occasionally (now more than ever) interrupted by Justin's supposed "practical jokes."

I didn't mind when Justin and one other person moved the contents of my locker and put it in another. I might point out that my lock is still missing to this day and has had to be replaced. I ignored him when he would knock my chair with his foot during class. I put up with day after day having to look in other desks for my pens. I was a little upset when he and one other student would hide my bag in another part of the school. But there is a point when I draw the line.

Today, March 31, I rode my bike to school and I locked it inside, but it wasn't locked to anything stationary. Well, in the middle of my French class, I was informed that somehow my bike was lying on the stairs in the entrance to the school. Justin later admitted he was responsible. Not only could he have caused damage to my bike, but people were having to walk over it while going up or down the stairs. Someone could have been hurt.

When Justin does these things, he often provokes other students as well. This really upsets me and at some points, I can't even concentrate on my work. All of this is making my stay at School very unpleasant. Please have a talk with your son.

I think Justin's problem is that he feels he has the right to hurt another human being. What gives him the right to assault another person, verbally, mentally and physically? This is not just recent behavior. It has been going on all year. It's not just the pranks but also his attitude. If he doesn't like me, then he should avoid me. The next time he attacks me, verbally or physically, I might not walk away; I might stand up to him, and the anger and tension that has built up may be released.

I have tried to talk to Justin, but it has not helped. I should also point out that I have in no way provoked any of the above mentioned supposed "practical jokes." I also mind when I'm punched, pushed and shoved by Justin, and I am sorry that it has come down to this.

I should inform you that a copy of this letter is being sent to each member of the school staff. I await a reply.

Peter Benton

Writing Memoirs and Biographies

When personal stories are developed and shared, young authors become aware that writing can reflect their lives. By linking personal experiences with their writing program, students find that their lives hold the potential for starting points for significant writing.

Julian created an image of himself in the future, an adolescent fantasy about his dreams.

A Day in Julian's Life

I saw Julian's light go on in his second floor apartment. His shadow appeared on the windows blinds. He must have now been in the kitchen, fixing something to eat.

The time was 9:30 p.m. Julian on that day was twenty-three years, three months and one day old. After eating his stale sandwich (half-finished) he switched on the television to catch the prime time television show of Simon V–Interviewer. He noticed after several minutes it was a rerun. Muttering something rude, he switched it off.

"Late again," he mumbled, making his way to the underground station. Getting off at Piccadilly, he climbed the steps up to the street and gave his ticket to the guard. Running through the rain, he made his way to his job. He walked through a gate with bold letters on it spelling RIEL PUB.

That night was going to be a hectic one. A Friday was traditionally busy particularly during the holiday at New Years. Julian was head bartender at the RIEL. Many of the RIEL's famous concoctions were his own, created in his early years in the business. Tonight Julian expected there to be at least 350 customers. The RIEL's capacity was 250. Hopefully, tonight he would have no surprise visits from the health department.

Occasionally when the bar slowed down or he had extra help at the counter, he would jam with the RIEL's hired band. Julian at the time was playing piano. However, he was once a professional guitarist and played with many of the well accomplished bands in the mid 1990s. However, he gave up the music scene, after creating for himself quite a reputation – to pursue a different career.

New Years, he unfortunately hadn't anytime to jam with the band, but he had been approached about a month beforehand with the proposition to record with the popular jazz fusion artist Cal Malhoon – the Irish musical ex-activist.

We need to encourage our students to tell the stories of their own lives. They can borrow the shapes and cadences, the words and phrases, of the professional authors they have read or that they have heard read aloud by generous parents and teachers. A student's identity, culture and origins may be revealed in each story told, and the resulting experience will give the original tale a pattern and texture that will enrich both the teller and the told. We can strengthen the students' story lives with the following activities.

✓ Make the classroom a safe place and a starting point for sharing life tales.

✓ Encourage spontaneous personal storytelling on each occasion when it is appropriate.

✓ Ask students to connect their own experiences to what they have read about or listened to.

✓ Use special events (a touring play, a professional storyteller, a visiting guest) as an occasion for sharing memories stimulated by the experience.

✓ Allow time for students to recount life stories formally during current events, or informally on rainy day recesses or at cleanup times.

✓ Use polished life tales as building blocks for personal writing, for painting or inside the safety of role playing in a drama lesson.

✓ Help students to use real-life stories as the basis for their fiction creations, both strengthening the believability of their writing and offering them a means for handling sensitive issues.

✓ Design opportunities for deep listening to the stories of others with a visit to a home for senior citizens or a hospice.

✓ Arrange for sharing stories with a buddy class of different-aged students in the school, or have a local high-school class come and tell polished life tales about their years in elementary grades.

✓ Tell your own life tales from both your teaching world and your personal life to strengthen or model a point that arises during a discussion or a shared reading. Swapping tales is still the best way of motivating your students to tell their stories.

There are many biographies by authors who write for young people, and these can be useful as both reading resources for your students and as opportunities for exploring viewpoints about the art of writing:

A Girl from Yamhill by Beverly Cleary
Boy: Tales of Childhood by Roald Dahl
The Abracadabra Kid: A Writer's Life by Sid Fleischman
Childtimes by Eloise Greenfield and Lessie Jones Little
On Writing: A Memoir of the Craft by Stephen King
Little by Little by Jean Little
Looking Back by Lois Lowry
Bad Boy by Walter Dean Myers
Guts: The True Stories Behind Hatchet and the Brian Books by Gary Paulsen
Knots in My Yo-yo String by Jerry Spinelli

Life Stories at a Secondary School

Michael Rossetti is a teacher enrolled in our graduate educational program. His work is focusing on building strategies for bringing authentic literacy events into the lives of his students. He writes:

> Our life-stories project, which began in April, seemed to me a meaningful and worthwhile activity for all—students and staff. It would allow everyone to share, listen to, write, and read stories. Our short-term goal was to engage the graduating class by publishing their stories in a booklet that they would receive in June as a memento of their high-school years. The long-term project was the publication of life stories—a sampling of stories representing students in each grade, teaching staff, administration, and office and custodial staffs.

And they achieved their goal. Their booklet of life tales is full of stories of the joys and problems of adolescents, and many teachers shared their own contributions.

During follow-up discussions, teachers remarked how important their own stories were to their students, both in the sharing and in the writing stages. Writing became contagious when students saw their teachers writing their own stories. One teacher, in particular, commented that "people began to get involved once they saw that I was willing to be the risk taker."

Student questionnaires provided interesting feedback. Both males and females enjoyed most the sharing and telling of stories. Clearly, the most difficult aspect of the storytelling week was the selection of a topic to write about. Writing out their stories posed the next greatest problem. A smaller percentage of both males and females said that "leaving things out which could not be shared" and "sharing your story" were the least difficult. For the males, sad moments, most embarrassing moments and personal experiences were topics that many did not want to talk or write about. Females listed school, family and personal relationships as problematic topics. One boy stated that "writers can use metaphor to tell their story." Surprisingly, a number of boys expressed how these stories help them express their feelings and thus give them an opportunity to reflect on their own lives and make it easier to "open up to people."

This story booklet was extremely well received by both students and staff, and Michael says that it was a beautiful sight to see one hundred graduates intently reading their stories during the grad luncheon: "I have been fortunate to be involved in such a life-giving process."

One of the life stories from their booklet that I particularly enjoyed was Anthony's:

Kiss the Cook

Eggs, flour, sugar and water. These are the main ingredients to my secrets. Throughout high school, we learned many things, including math, algebra, science, history, and all our friends' secrets. Mine (if you have not tasted it yet), is cooking, or to be exact, baking. My secret came out in grade ten, during French class. It was the week before Christmas holidays, and I, being such a nice guy, decided to bring Ms Palozzi some of the cookies my family bakes for Christmas. We are Italian, and everyone knows that around the holidays our house is full of goodies. As a result of a simple plate of cookies, I ended up with an interesting reputation that would stay with me for the rest of my high school career.

From that day forward, Christmas would be a time everyone in my school would remember, especially my teachers. I just wanted to bring cookies to thank my teachers for a job well done. These lucky recipients included Ms Paris, Ms Goveia, Ms D'Avella, Mrs DiConstanzo (for whom I also baked my famous torrone for her daughter's communion), and the list goes on and on.

Eventually my friends found out and became a little jealous (Alberto), and I had to bake for them too, and even their mothers (Patrick). Not many people enjoy baking when they find it so easy to go to a store and buy ready-made cakes and cookies. I have one question for you critics: Would you really enjoy doing what I do? Do you want to get your hands covered in dough as you mix it with your hands and not some mixer? That is what I enjoy so much! Baking is part of my life, and it will stay with me for ever. Without baking, I would be...thin. Every good chef must taste his goodies before he gives them away. I need baking as a form of relaxation. It makes me happy and others too. Baking is my hobby (doing dishes not included), and I am good at it and proud of it. Not too many people can cook (I am not naming names). I have a specialty that is hard to beat (no pun intended), and unlike Martha Stewart, I bake my things myself.

During my years at high school, I have done many things that have added to my reputation, and who knows? The next time the smell of freshly baked cookies roams through the halls, it might be one of my "special deliveries."

Writing from our Reading

Connecting our writing with our reading seems to make sense to me. Of course, no matter the topic, we are always borrowing the bits of craft we remember from the books we have read. It is how writers grow. For years, I separated reading and writing in my teaching. Now I recognize the connections we can make to enable our students to find ideas in the texts they experience that may inspire them to write their own responses or to compose in a similar genre or format. Simon was a student of mine who was fascinated by the language Robert Newton Peck used in his book *A Day No Pigs Would Die*. He created this monologue for the character Pinky:

Hello, ma name is Pinky, – and ah'm a pig. From what I kin gather, I was Mr. Tanner's until Robert – he's ma master and friend – gone done himself some heroic deed. I understand that he did born Mr. Tanner's calves – Bob and Bib, and that did rip-out a goiter, all by himself. He got pretty torned up, so Mr. Tanner gave me to him. I kin just remember that April day when Mr. Tanner gone stuck we in his coat and took me off to Robert's. I didn't know the heck was going on. Everythin' was alright though, once I was in Robert's hands. His body was as warm as my mama's underside, and I could feel the love jest seeping out of every little hole. I decided to lick his face, jest to let him know that the feelin' was mutual. All of sudden, Robert started to callin' me Pinky – I didn't know any better, so's I went along with it. Robert, Mr. Tanner, and Mr. Peck – Robert's father – talked for a time, all the while Robert was squeezing me, – what love! Eventually Mr. Tanner left, and I was put down on the ground. This was a new experience for me. I'd never been on this ground before. I was a bit scared, an' very cautious. I sniffed at Robert's heel, and cuddled up against his leg, I wanted Robert's 'fection – I was scared.

Later on that day, I eyed myself a restin' spot – a beautiful crib. It was made of wood, and lined with straw. If only mama could've seen it. Rob and Mr. Peck were fussing all over the darned thing, but I liked it just the way it was. When night fell, I was very tired, so much had happened that day, and so quickly! Robert picked me up and put me inside my new home – it was like a palace – pig heaven. Rob, then cuddled down beside me. I loved it, I was warm, comfortable, loved, and wanted – I decided I was gonna like this place. Well, that was my first day with the Pecks, – just one thing troubled me; what was a Shaker???

I tried the same idea with a group of student teachers; each had read a young-adult novel as a means of sharing their books with others and adding to our repertoire of books for young people. When they read aloud their monologues to group members, I recognized the talent these young teachers would have to share with their students, and I felt strengthened by the voices they had created from their reading and from their lives. We can celebrate teachers as writers.

How far away these occasions are from writing the book report, which is actually a testing device rather than a teaching strategy. If the reports the student wrote were an outgrowth of the reading and the subsequent reflection that grew from conversations with fellow readers about the text, or from thoughtful reflections drawn from the student's reading journal, then these could help students consider the text in light of the experiences surrounding it—a far cry from "I liked it" or "I didn't like it." How rich their own writing becomes when they see their ideas in print, watching what they thought they knew change and alter in the moment through the very act of writing. The qualities of the powerful texts they read—the words, the style, the issues, the alternative points of view—offer them added strength for constructing their own arguments and meaning-making compositions. They begin to notice and perhaps appreciate the art of writing, where words crafted with care and compassion can create an aesthetic and intellectual response to issues of the human condition.

Writing Instructions

As a genre, written instructions require a different construct from other written forms of organizing information. Because readers need to follow the ideas presented carefully, writers can receive important feedback information that will affect revision. Steve Hurley is a school consultant focusing on information technology, and has collected some interesting examples of instructional writing involving the computer:

> Recognizing the power of Information Technology to help students develop the ability to write, read and follow instructions in an interactive way, junior teachers at a Brampton School are embarking on a project which uses the Internet in an innovative way. Grade 5 students at one school use a computer drawing application to create a picture of their dream house. While the house can be as large or as small as they wish, it must be comprised of closed geometrical shapes. After completing their creations, they are then required to write a set of instructions designed to allow another student to reproduce their work. The instructions are e-mailed to students at a partner school who use them to recreate the picture. These students then e-mail

their version of the dream house back to the original authors. The original instructions and picture, as well as the partner's reproduction, are posted to the project web site for discussion.

A few years ago, while working on a genre study involved with reading and writing instructions, I asked the eighth-grade students to remember a time when they wished they had had an instructional manual of some type to help them with a task that had caused them some difficulty. Philip, who had been working with me renovating a house, decided to incorporate that experience into his writing.

How to Remove Plaster from a Wall

I'm going to discuss three major parts of this time-consuming job: preparing, removing and other problems of removing plaster from a brick wall.

The first and most important thing you should do is cover everything with plastic. The dust is terrible.

Next, make sure you've got a pair of safety goggles and a safety mask. The goggles are used to protect your eyes from small bits of plaster. It's painful and takes forever to get particles of plaster out. It is also harmful to your eyes. The mask is used to keep the dust out of your lungs. The best masks are the type with changeable filters. The only thing you might want to wear is a hat to keep plaster out of your hair.

What do you use to remove the plaster? Your hands? Maybe.

However, the best tool to use is a regular hammer. Do not use a sledge hammer. They are too heavy to swing. The weight slows it down and you'll just mark the wall. And even if you are able to get a good swing you will most likely put a hole in your wall. Wooden-handled hammers are better than rubber-handled hammers; they won't cause your hands to blister.

Now you're ready to start. You swing the hammer, hit the wall and nothing happens. Why? The easiest way to remove the plaster is by angling the hammer when you make contact with the wall. It doesn't matter where you start. Once you get going it becomes very easy. Hint: it's best to hit the wall about five inches from the previous blow; the plaster should come off faster.

The only problem with this task is if you plan to play baseball the next day; you'll find out it's quite painful to pick up anything, such as a bat. There is no way to avoid this problem. Your hands will be the same as usual after a couple of days.

So the best of luck in your task. One other thing I should mention: if you ever work for a man named Booth, and he wants you to do some plaster removal, he'll probably tell you it's a two-hour job. Don't believe a word of it. The job will most likely take you at least six hours.

Reporting and Giving Opinions

Writing reports, articles and editorials offer young people opportunities for incorporating both information and their own personal perspectives and viewpoints into their writing projects. They can collect data and observations about issues and concerns that interest them in their school lives and in their community, and then add their own comments using their own voice. Informed opinion is the heart of an effective column, and students in the middle years are certainly ready at the drop of a hat to share their opinions on almost any topic. Sharing this type of writing often results in useful feedback, and the original ideas continue to develop and grow. We can use these types of activities as sources for their writing projects, working toward two basic goals: the need for informed opinion, and the struggle to become aware of the differences between fact and opinion. These are especially difficult areas as there are so many different viewpoints about contemporary issues. However, we can find many instances where opinion writing can be useful to developing writers: advertisements and commercials, reviews, letters, advice columns, speeches, editorials and debates. The Internet can be invaluable as a resource for examining complex issues, and of course for providing grounds for discussing the factual validity of the information. Sharing reviews about the books the students are reading allows for critical writing and promotes new books for others to read.

Entered in a contest for writing in a school student newspaper, Jeff's report won an award. Originally, he used a pseudonym as protection from embarrassment, but time strengthens us, and he shares his winning entry right out front:

The Day the Laughter Died

Apologies to all the females reading this, but you couldn't possible understand. You don't know how it feels. It's bad. Really bad! It is the worst possible sports injury imaginable. Not, it's not a Charlie Horse. Nope, it's not a concussion. It's not even a facial laceration. This injury is the reason sports players wear athletic supporters, jocks, or cups. This injury is commonly known as the groin injury.

I can empathize with all those hockey players who forgot to wear their athletic supporters that one time, the one time the puck seemed to hit them in the ever sensitive 'bathing suit area.' I can empathize with the baseball players who had to go behind the plate for an inning because the catcher was out with a concussion. Unfortunately, the player wasn't wearing a cup, and oops, the ball bounced off the plate and 'he goes down for the count.' I can even empathize with the football player who goes deep in the end zone in the mild touch-football game. The ball is traveling right into his hands for the game winning play when the defender knocks the ball down into his midsection. Ouch!

There are an infinite number of possibilities for the cause of the injury, but there is only one reaction. First, there is the realization that 'the section' was hit; "Gee, this is embarrassing, and this is going to hurt right about … NOW!" Then, there is a scream louder than a high-pitched piccolo followed by double-over in pain. Next comes a longer term effect – a voice that is sucking in helium for the next couple of hours. The area remains tender for days, or weeks, or even months. There is no surgery, no medication, and no relief for the abominable 'groinal concussion.' There is just pain – lots of pain.

Movie and television comedies often feature some parody of this worst possible sports injury which almost guarantees a laugh from the audience. The injured, however, will never laugh again, until maybe some distant future when he is fully recovered. Until that heavenly time, there is nothing funny about not being able to walk. With no hyperbole intended, the groin injury feels like the entrance to hell with the devil waiting to admit all of the criminals in the world.

The injury may not happen very often, but when it does, the pain is felt vicariously by all (male) spectators in stadiums and hockey rinks. Pro sports almost never see this injury occur but when it does the player can be guaranteed a spot on a highlight reel.

If you happen to be one of those lucky guys who has never suffered the 'injury,' go buy a lottery ticket. One day, it may happen to you and that will be the day that the laughter died.

Jeff Swartz

The students in Nancy's class must participate in a community service project during the year. Their experiences serve as significant resources for their independent writing projects. This student was working with the organization Meals on Wheels, and described his first visit with a client:

Henry

"Kablaaaam!!!!" I stood up straight to ease my back. These trays were not light.

After all the trays were organized, the checklists double confirmed, the groups assembled, the routes overlooked and everyone
quiet, there were orders from the director to collect our trays and
head out to our cars.

Once we were settled in Sammy's 2000 silver Hyundai two-door
sedan, we headed out to deliver lunches. Our first delivery was to a
man named Henry. The short trip there was filled with a good laugh
when Sammy and Frank started popping jokes at each other. They
were funny guys; all was going well, but the laughter was about to
stop...

I didn't know what to expect walking up the eroded steps with a
tray and a small carton of milk in my free hand. Frank came with me
and as we approached the door Frank said, "Zis iz a very sad man."

I looked at the front of the house before knocking on the door.
There was a rotting piece of plywood that was peeling from the
façade and there were a noticeable number of cracks and holes in
his thick wooden door. There was no handle on the door just a
nailed piece of two-by-four.

Frank stepped forwards and knocked on the door. "Klunk, klunk!"
There was a pause, then the door was opened. There stood a man,
around 50 years old. He was wearing a pair of oversized dirty blue
sweatpants, help up by a piece of yarn. He had on a stained white
and blue striped dress shirt that was missing half of its buttons. His
hair was greyish brown and it was long (shoulder-length) and mat-
ted. He looked like a skeleton because his face was very pale and
bony.

"Hi, there!" he exclaimed.

"Hello. Come in please, Come in," he said in a very weak voice.

As Frank and I entered, we were blanketed with darkness. We
were standing in a short, skinny hallway that led to a staircase. To
our left was a wall. To our right there was a dark room in which I
could make out a foldout couch with a thin blanket on it. It was very
cold and I doubted whether he had any heaters, or if he even had
electricity.

I handed him the lunch tray and the milk and he thanked me with a
kind voice. "Goodbye," said Frank, as we stepped outside into the
cool winter air.

"Goodbye," Henry replied, as he shut his paper-thin door and
retreated to his cold, musty, foldout couch bed.

We returned to Sammy's 2000 silver Hyundai two door sedan and
drove away.

Writing Fiction

I had just finished reading the latest mystery novel by P. D. James on the airplane to Vancouver. Having read them all, I am still intrigued by her storytelling power, strengthened by her background in forensic science, her acute observations of life in present-day England and her carefully crafted characterizations of every major and minor character. I have been to many cathedrals and abbeys in Great Britain, and when she describes one (she insists from her imagination), I am transported overseas for the moment, although the corpse in the sanctuary is usually missing on my trips.

Of course, writing fiction is a complex task, especially for young people. Donald Graves in *A Fresh Look at Writing* sums up the difficulties:

> Most of the fiction that children write reflects their impression of what fiction is like. They want their stories to be exciting. Thus, their focus is on high-speed events reminiscent of Saturday morning cartoons. Older children choose bizarre and violent chases, space shootings, or war with modern weapons. (p. 287)

But then, most of the fiction they experience in their own worlds represents this style of plot-driven action. Teachers, by offering them other models in their reading, and by having mini-lessons that focus on the attributes of effective fiction writing, may be able to move their fiction writing into new areas.

I am always attempting to find ways of helping young writers create fiction that is more than a series of plottings. Graves says that the secret may lie in giving the students strategies for developing characters who in the writing are beginning "to understand other people, themselves, and the human condition" (p. 288).

✓ Mini-lessons on developing characters can involve reading excerpts from fiction they have enjoyed, writing that talks about why a character behaves as he did, what in the character's life led to this action. Reflective narrative plays a large part in fiction writing, and can present to students a means of deepening their own work.

✓ You can build with the students a life web of a character from a story they have shared; all of the events that happened, what the character felt and the motivations behind the actions.

✓ Learning about fiction happens in small doses. Short passages are more effective for students to write than long twenty-page epics. Ralph Fletcher gives some very helpful strategies in his book *What a Writer Needs*.

✓ During a conference, you can engage the student in developing his or her work orally with you, discussing why the character is behaving in that way, wondering aloud what had happened in the character's life in the past or asking for clarification for details that would paint a clearer picture.

✓ Writing in other formats, such as poetry, short scripts or fictional memoirs, can help young writers gain a sense of how fiction works, as they move from their imaginations to putting their ideas into words.

Much of my own work has been in exploring the themes and situations of a story with dramatic role playing. It seems to me this is a particularly useful way to look at fiction writing. If youngsters' responses to their reading lead to unanswered or ambiguous questions, then there may be opportunities for the students to write about the happenings between the lines or the unwritten scenes. But what drives my own work with students are the analogous or parallel worlds that can be created alongside those in the story. What would another character do in a similar situation? How might a different action change the course of events in the new telling? As they consider the twists their questions bring to what they had read, students can create a new story on the shoulders of the original.

Writing Poetry

On the evening of my son's graduation from eighth grade, I found him awake in bed at one in the morning, reading the yearbook from his grades seven and eight. It was a collection of writings from their writing workshops that the teacher Nancy Steele had collated into a booklet, but what Jay was reading and rereading represented the lives of the classmates he had been with for those two years. Their writings were mainly poems, and somehow Nancy had been able, in her carefully structured program, to offer this genre to her students as a means of capturing their very beings at this stage of adolescence. The emotional swings, the shocking observations of the adult world, the new awareness of strong feelings—all seem to fit inside the shapes of poetry that she modeled and shared with them. The following samples are from this year's booklet, and they make me want to find a class and read and write nothing but poetry for the next two years.

Cottage Morning

Small familiar sounds create
the sounds of nothing
ripples over the smooth lake
the water – almost like ice
so perfect and black
undisturbed.
I descend the stairs
creaky and slippery
from the night's sleep
rocks and pebbles roll
under my bare feet
step onto the water
my foot makes rings
of indignation
the water freezes my skin
runs up my leg

Walnut

brown and wrinkled
smooth in the palm of my hand
it protects itself
resisting my attempts
to pry it open –
until it shatters
and shards of sharp shell
fly everywhere.

Alberta

The edge of a prairie town
        looking into the empty sun...
i see an empty playground,
        swings clank together in the slight breeze
        a rusty maypole sits
        calmly, quietly, waiting
        the slide stands tall and proud,
metal glinting in the sunset
i hear the sizzle of hot pavement
        the singing of hot pavement
i smell the silence and emptiness
        the heat baking the ground

i taste my lips, dry and salty
        the warmth of the prairie air
i feel the glow of my burning face
        grass tickling my leg —
        playing and dancing at my feet
i am glad to be here,
        and i collect my broken thoughts
        and enjoy the moment
        standing on the prairie sunset.

Mystery Object

My great-grandfather's watch
Smells faintly of cigars and brandy
Staring into its golden surface I see my reflection
Along with that of my grandfather, and his father before him
Though cared for on its long journey
It shows signs of erosion on the delicate silver knobs
Thousands of hours contained in its weary metal hands
It has become a grandfather
Wiser than the modern-day contraption
It now
Is time itself.

Classmates

I sit in class, pondering an assignment I cannot execute.
I look around.
Cedric sits, having a staring contest with his eraser,
oblivious to the worksheet deathtrap
surrounding him
Zach is having an argument with his own mind about what to put in his
latest story
he just ends up asking Cedric
Leith is not talking to anyone, but his facial expression suggests:
touch me and die
a devilish proud-type smile crosses his mind
I think
I wonder if he wants to play BROOD today?
Drew is making another stupid comment
a wave in the ocean
soon to be silenced
"Shut up, Drew."

that was Alix
classic example of, uhh....
something.
Jacob is funny, in a cynical sense.
I become weary of observing these primates
I retire to my work.

Writing Scripts

Even with all the attention popular culture gives the media, script writing seldom appears in our writing programs. It may be thought of as too complex an
activity, like writing a novel, but there are dozens of types of scripts we could
consider. We need to decide if the work the students create is to be read aloud,
or if the dialogue is simply a useful format around which we can structure our
ideas, as in a poem where the writer wants to isolate two voices.

Script writing is one of the best activities I have found for causing students to
revise. It is not easy to write words that others can then give life to. If you can
create a process where the writers observe their words being spoken aloud and
then both hear and see the need for revision, the writing process is truly authentic.

Transforming a text selection into script dialogue involves students in several
literacy processes. For example, selecting part of a novel and turning the narrative into dialogue forces careful reading of the text, and requires the writer to
interpret the prose, maintaining the intent of the story and the characters while
presenting the thoughts and actions through dialogue.

✓ A page or two is usually enough text to write and revise. Partners could
   work on a short story, attempting to transform it into a script. (How much
   narrative will they retain? How will they externalize the thoughts of the
   characters?) Then groups can exchange stories for reading aloud and sharing.

✓ Conversations that have been taped are good sources for scripting. An
   improvised scene can be transformed into a script for others to read aloud.
   It is important to keep the scenes brief: transcribing is hard work but, as
   James Moffett indicated, these are perfect occasions for observing how the
   conventions of print work, as recorded speech has to be represented in
   print.

✓ A conversation recorded from a book club or a literature circle can be an
   excellent resource for transcribing into script. Students can select a significant moment in the discussion to be transcribed, and the resulting dia-

logue can be used by the group to analyze their contribution to the understanding of their novel. This can benefit both the students and the teacher.

✓ We should support those students who enjoy choosing this format for some of their writing projects. Philip was a devoted fan of the TV show M*A*S*H and, after reading a published collection of scripts from the show, decided to write his own. He carefully followed the style of the originals, and yet created his own very funny contribution in which the character Klinger, a man who wears women's clothes, attends a Halloween party in which everyone else is dressed like a woman except him; he is in a male's costume. Philip's work was a fully realized script that other students enjoyed reading.

✓ In Nancy Steele's class, all students participate in a script writing process. The students then select twelve of the completed projects, cast them and produce them for a parents' night. During that evening, plays are presented in three different rooms at the same time, as in a three-ring circus, and the visitors can select four of them to watch. I have had the pleasure of attending three of her play nights, and I am always amazed at the level of writing and acting in these student-produced, and informally-presented scripts.

Writing in Role

Drama can support writing activities, from reflective journals and letters, to interviews and proclamations. It also provides opportunities for collective writing, in which groups collaborate on a mutual enterprise—cooperating in collecting data, organizing information, revising and editing—to be used in the subsequent drama work. If they are engaged in the expressive and reflective aspects of drama, living through "here and now" experiences that draw upon their own life meanings, then the writing that accompanies the drama and the writing that grows out of it may possess the same characteristics and qualities.

Writing inside a drama context, the students begin to think of themselves as writers, controlling the medium in order to find a way to say what they want to say to people they want to reach. Because writing may be used within the drama and may be read or listened to by others, there is a built-in reason to proofread and edit.

Writing out of role, or as a result of having been in role, lets students enter a new sphere of attitudes and feelings. As they try for a more complex imaginative understanding of what has happened in their drama, their writing often becomes more intense.

Writing in role allows learners to write in new forms:

proclamations	first-person accounts	biographies
speeches	petitions	commentaries
diaries	monologues	newspaper articles
lyrics/songs	interviews	announcements

I was working with a fourth-grade class and their teacher, Franca, reading the picture book *Coyote Winter*. The students had explored in role the complications that had arisen when the teacher in the story had freed the coyote and angered the farmers. There were no simple answers in the work, but their sympathies remained with the coyote pup. Later in the week, they wrote these reflective monologues from their memories of the work.

I am coyote. I have lost my way.
Suddenly I saw a chicken in the snow. Of course, I was hungry.
I walked toward the chicken when I felt this sudden pain in my leg.
I looked down and saw some metal jaws digging into my skin.
I thought my life had ended. I lay down and waited for the hunters to come.
I felt sad and helpless. I thought about the warm den in the forest and I thought about my mother, who would wake up and start looking for me.
I had been lying for nearly an hour when I heard some voices.
Now I thought my time had come. But when I looked up I saw a woman with lots of students.
I was scared. To my surprise the woman was trying to free me.
When she did I licked her and tried to do something to make her understand that I was trying to thank her.
But the students chased me away.
At first I did not understand. Finally, I understood. Danger was near.
So I left. But I was sad.
I had lost my mother and didn't have anybody to take care of me.
I roamed the forest for the rest of my life keeping away from man.

Simon

I am a coyote and I hurt.
My paw is numb, my leg is sore and tingly.
I licked my wounds but will they heal?
I am hungry but do I dare go in search of food?
I should go back to the den – perhaps mother will help me.
I must be careful.

103

I thought the world would be an interesting place. A place to explore and play.
Now it is a frightening place; problems exist for me that I hadn't thought of before.
I must be cautious, play less, move carefully.
I wonder if my leg will heal before other animals find that I am hurt.

Franca (teacher)

Curriculum Connections

Students are writing throughout the day in school. If we take note of what and how they are writing, we can learn a great deal about their strategies as writers. The following examples of student writing demonstrate the amount and variety of written work that can occur in the different curriculum areas.

In her book *The Write Math*, Cathy Marks Krpan demonstrates the many and varied occasions there are in the teaching of mathematics for us to involve students in writing, assess their literacy growth and work alongside them.

> The student was asked to explain the difference between perimeter and surface.
>
> "The difference between perimeter and surface area is a lot different. Perimeter is the distance around the side of an object, and surface area is the area, or size of the inside of the shape. So, here is a diagram of the two. Perimeter is also done for a flat shape or side, whereas surface area is done on a 3D object."
>
> Kristen is in eighth grade. She integrates mathematical sketches to help clarify what she is writing. After reading her explanation, Kristen's teacher responded in writing to Kristen's exploration, "You have provided several examples to explain the difference between the two concepts. One question I have is how can surface area be used to measure the size of the inside of a shape?
>
> Kristen responded back in writing that she meant that it is used to measure the surface area of each face of a three-dimensional shape. She then added this point to her writing exploration. (p. 24)

Simon collected autographs as his hobby. His major writing project in ninth grade concerned his hobby, and his foreword to his extensive piece of work sets the scene.

When the majority of people think of authography collecting, they look down their noses and only think of the teenage groupies that hang around outside the airports or sports arenas awaiting their favorite athlete or rock star.

They fail to realize that the majority of serious collectors are very reputable members of society, who are responsible for the preservation of historical documents. If it weren't for autograph collectors – or philographers – many many periods of history would be a mystery, due to the fact that the only link between the present and the past in many cases is writing.

I am sure, that at one time or another, all of us have acquired at least one autograph. Whether it be a book signed by the author, or photo signed by a celebrity, or just a scrap of paper bearing the signature of a local politician of person of notoriety. Who could honestly say that when they were growing up, they wouldn't have loved an autographed photo of the Beatles, or their favorite rock or movie star, or some other person or persons that they idolized.

Even though there isn't a terrifically wide range of serious collectors – Philography is one of the oldest hobbies. Long before the Penny Black came onto the scene, people were signing their names, and others were saving them. You are about to learn that there is an awful lot more to autographs than groupies!!!

Julian chose to describe his corner store as part of a unit on a neighborhood study.

To begin with I haven't got a corner store. The closest franchise which resembles a corner store is Moore Milk, which I never go to. However I have been to McDonalds, which is – yes, on a corner. This one is on the corner of Yonge and St. Clair. Conveniently built on the same block as two cinemas and junior high school. On the other side of Yonge is a second rate mall. Its shops are expensive yet always crowded with customers – browsers. To the north and around the corner of Mac's one will find the beginnings of sunny Forest Hill.

That corner is usually busy. Even on the coldest day you can find people going in and out of McDonalds. Most of the characters there are moviegoers, before or after their evening at the flicks they come in pairs or in groups of three or four. Most of them are in their late teens or early twenties.

In the evening people stand outside and joke about going in, saying "Golly, we're all going out to eat at McDonalds." Little kids pass by with their parents or grandmother, licking on their Baskin Robin's goop. Plop – Billy spilt ice cream on his alligator!

Midsummer, Mac's seems to fit in the musty atmosphere. There's something about Mac's in a summer evening. The people are few. You get your odd group of urban cowboys – joking about their spending spree in Mac's. You have your odd bum, and of course – the usual extremely incompetent and silly looking cashier. Ah, the joylessness of Mac's. The thing is, it's so nice to sit there, amongst all that plastic. One feels a kinship with others in there. We all know it's garbage were eating, but everyone does it, so it must be alright.

McDonalds has had the pleasure of my visits on more than one occasion. To sum it up, we love to hate McDonalds, and it's better in the summer there because you can sit and hate the place in warmth.

Planning, Researching and Writing Projects

Anne Lamott's heartfelt treatise on the world of writing, *Bird by Bird*, offers very clear instructions for school projects:

> Thirty years ago my older brother, who was ten years old at the time, was trying to get a report on birds written that he'd had three months to write. It was due the next day. We were out at our family cabin in Bolinas, and he was at the kitchen table close to tears, surrounded by binder paper, and pencils, and unopened books on birds, immobilized by the hugeness of the task ahead. Then my father sat down beside him, put his arm around my brother's shoulder, and said: "Bird by bird, Buddy. Just take it bird by bird."

There are many jokes about parents researching and writing the projects their students are assigned. Our classrooms have come a long way from demanding that projects submitted without our guidance be artistically beautiful creations often relying on parental support. Now we see them as in-depth writing projects that demonstrate the students' high-level learning in both content and process, and that offer them opportunities for teaching others about what they have discovered. If we want students to develop as young writers, it is important to help them set up a system that enables them to experience the learning that grows from a project personally, so that they acquire skills of handling information. While parents may assist by providing data, by offering to be interviewed or by helping publish the final drafts, the students need to have ownership of their work.

Most importantly, students need to write their own researched information using a particular pattern or genre, incorporating the structure of the print text into their own work, constructing and comprehending the genre at the same time. We can help youngsters come to grips with assigned projects and papers, so that they are not left to flounder, but gradually accumulate the strategies necessary for working with a variety of genres of information.

Student inquiries and investigations can grow from a topic or an issue drawn from the students' own interests and questions that stimulate their curiosity and cause them to want to find answers or solutions. Research can grow from science or social studies as well, or from the themes in novels and picture books. These inquiries can last for a few days or several weeks. Some aspects may be covered as homework, but the classroom is the best place for identifying a topic, formulating questions and developing a plan of research. Intensive long-term research projects immerse the students in authentic reading and writing experiences, and we can help maintain their interests and sustain their efforts.

Students often need help in planning how to structure the information they have found through their research inquiry. We can help them with ways to sort, select and arrange their data by conducting mini-lessons. Examples of student writing we collect often give them frames for organizing their own investigations. Rather than demanding outlines for writing projects, we need to offer guidance and models for building effective structures. In the end, we want to be able to see what they have learned through their intensive research writing, and the results should document their growth.

Occasions in which students present their inquiries offer opportunities for both oral communication and written and visual demonstrations of the research. I am impressed by the power of overhead transparencies to cause students to carefully consider how they will represent their findings. In some schools, they can move into presentations using the computer. Displays and bulletin boards let other students benefit from the research, and young investigators may want to distribute a guide sheet for observers to note their learning and to ask further questions.

Evaluation rubrics are useful for letting the students reflect on their learning processes, and for recording the types of writing and research they explore. This is a good opportunity for setting up standards that actually affect how others will view the work: using media effectively; representing the information neatly with careful handwriting or computer printing; arranging the graphic display artistically; using captions and headings to stimulate interest and to give cohesion to the study.

Having completed an in-depth study of a topic of interest means the students will have explored the types of writing that will be valuable throughout their school years and in their future lives, engaging in authentic inquiries in order to discover and communicate their findings. It may be the first time students recognize that the process of writing occurs in the content subjects, and that they need to see themselves as readers and writers when they are involved in subject disciplines. Literacy does not only raise its head in language arts; it is a life-long interpreting and constructing process.

✓ Students can gain help from each other by sharing their initial questions with a partner or a small study group, breaking the topic into bite-sized chunks, helping with categories and headings, suggesting other resources, offering support with the presentation of the information—how to inform others with text and graphics or how to connect the different sections to create an overview.

✓ Data can be collected in notebooks, on file cards, charts, transparencies, clipboards or stick-it notes; can be captured on recorders, cameras and video cameras; can be summarized on computer disks, photocopies, drawings and diagrams.

✓ Searching the Internet and web sites can provide a rich data bank for locating information. However, the material is often unreferenced and there are unsuitable sites. With guidance, the electronic search can open up worlds of knowledge to young researchers. Appropriate software, CD ROMs, videotapes and films can give students access to information, often in a dramatic documentary form. For example, a group of students can preview several videotapes on a monitor set up in the hallway.

✓ Students can conduct interviews which, when recorded and then summarized or transcribed, offer primary source data to support an inquiry. Besides in-person interviews, students can conduct conversations on the phone, by e-mail or on a chat line on the computer. Authors are not always available for interviews, but there are printed conversations sometimes available in journals or in books about writers. It may be just as significant to interview people who experienced the incident described in a novel; a man who spent his life working in a mine may have as much to say as the writer of a book about mining.

✓ First-hand research sites can include another classroom, libraries, a field trip location such as a museum or science centre, government buildings, a theatre group or a shopping mall.

✓ Research inquiries can lead to a variety of other print resources: magazine and newspaper articles, manuals and guides, brochures and catalogues. Students will have real reasons for using references such as the encyclopedia, all types of dictionaries, the *Guinness Book of World Records*, maps and atlases, telephone directories or statistics to support and substantiate their investigations.

✓ Documents offer special insights for research: letters and diaries, wills, archival photos, vintage books, land deeds and surveys, reproduced or downloaded from the Internet.

✓ Students may become aware through research of the amazing variety of nonfiction books that are written on almost every topic. Using the catalogue files at the library, scanning the stacks or conducting a web search can locate resources that can lead to intensive and deep reading experiences.

✓ Fiction is also a research source when investigating an author, issue or historical setting. Comparing picture books or novels read by group members presents a different type of data. For example, the students can map out an area of land that was described in a nonfiction book. They can include a key to forested areas, and mark lakes, rivers and other topographical information.

✓ Students can use the information they know about the topic to create a web or a chart. They can record their findings in a variety of formats: definitions, directories, recipes, manuals, dictionaries, explanations, alphabet books, memos, newspapers, letters, summaries, reviews, television guides, instructions, atlases, reports, articles, announcements, journals.

It is often useful to have the students reflect on their research experiences by writing about the books or other resources they have read as they prepared or observations they had made, perhaps discussing new facts they have learned or problems they have experienced while researching.

Nancy Steele's class in downtown Toronto engaged in a three-month unit called Facing History, based on the equity and diversity components of a curriculum document, and focusing on the Holocaust of World War II and the resulting emigration of survivors to North America. The issues in this theme are complex and difficult. I had the fortunate opportunity of watching the class at work for much of the time, planning with and observing the teacher in action, role playing with the students on occasion and documenting the language processes used by the students throughout the three months. The talk, the writing and the reading of these eighth-grade youngsters gave rise to the writing samples that follow.

A library of novels concerned with the Holocaust had been set up during the previous month in Nancy's classroom, and many students had read several of the books. The class watched a documentary film, *America and the Holocaust*, about an American who as a young man emigrated from Germany and then tried to bring his parents to America to escape the Holocaust. This film provided background about this tragic event and helped establish the context for the work to follow. One of the students wrote this film review:

This movie was frightening because *my* understanding grew past what *you* read in books, past the imagination to the real thing. I know that this is someone who went there. The film was telling me this, that these are real pictures, that the person in front of me on the screen was there. We saw people standing as if they were dead, people beyond skinny. The narrator has seen his family thrown into one big grave and buried. To know that they have survived this horror means they must be the strongest people. When the movie was over the same feeling I had was printed on everyone's face around me. The silence was stunning.

The class then participated in a series of drama lessons concerning the customs interviews the immigrants who came after the war had to endure. When the drama was over, the students were asked to write, in role, a diary entry they intended to save for their grandchildren, in which they described how they felt before, during, and after the interviews. At the same time, the students in role as the immigration officers wrote letters to the head of Canada First, an actual historical organization, reporting on their first day at work. The role demanded that they accept being members of a group that, in history, had resented and resisted the immigrants. Here are some of the letters and journal entries.

Re: Immigration Duties on 11/03/46

On November third, nineteen-hundred-and-forty-six, I, Dr. Evelyn Darling MD, was at the Immigration Office for Canada First. My duties as Chief Medical Officer were to check passports for valid landed immigration status, supervise Dr. Marvinel Laurie, my assistant, and perform medical tests on patients and decide whether they passed the health test, thus being in fit condition, not incubating any unknown/ known diseases, and in perfect mental health.

Letter of Resignation

Dear Canada First,
I am deciding to resign from my duties as medical officer of immigration because I now realize that the health of my family and I are jeopardized. These immigrants are not like normal patients, they carry all sorts of diseases, that span from the unsanitary conditions they lived in. These conditions include polio, TB, Infectious Hepatitis and malaria; all of which could be transmitted in an airborne manner. Having two young students, I feel it is my responsibility to abandon work with these refugees and to take up private practice where these infections are not present. It has been a wretched

week. We can't pass the immigrants because even if they are clear of infection, they could be carriers of lethal agents that lie dormant in their gastronomical tract or have disorders such as anemia or nerve system damage from cerebrospinal meningitis, that Canada's health program can't pay for. Not only does my job pose a danger to my life, but legally I should not pass anyone of this low quality health rendering my job completely pointless.

The work from the first event established the context for the second part of the unit, creating a community in 1964 that is threatened by change. The students worked in role as families of those immigrants who had come to Toronto, using the research gleaned from the preparation and the experiences of the first experience. Instructions had been given to all the students by their teacher:

> You are concerned about the news of this neighborhood being demolished for the building of the munitions factory. Decide how you will best be able to stop this from happening.

One of the students wrote in role as the editor of the local newspaper and created a report about a drama lesson in which a meeting was held with participants speaking in the roles of the people they had researched. I became the spokesperson for the conglomerate building the munitions factory in this urban renewal project, working in role as well.

The Kensington Times November 29, 1964

News reached yesterday that the government is going to build a munitions plant in the Kensington core with a loss of about 30 – 50 businesses. The weapons made will be sold to the USA government to aid in the Vietnam War. The plant is scheduled to be built in 3 years time and blue prints are already in progress. Relocation of citizens will be put into action in the near future.

Public action is already being organized to defeat the idea of this plant. Mrs. Julia Ford, head of the Kensington Business Association is "appalled that the government could do this to the thriving market." The munitions plant will result in the closure of several area schools, pollution, and many health issues. However Mrs. Steele, leader of the Munitions Plant Project (MPP) denies that this project will do any long-term damage to the Kensington Community.

A community meeting was held yesterday afternoon at Kensington Community School at Bathurst and College. Mrs. Steele introduced herself, the chairman and his associates, and talked about the need for a meeting. Mrs. Steele said she hoped to bring the suggestions back to the mayor.

Business leader J. J. Ford was the first speaker and expressed explicit concern over the relocation of businesses. The location of the plant was discussed but no locations were revealed. A local rabbi was deeply concerned about property values and the synagogue which may be destroyed.

The meeting was adjourned and we all stomped out of there with malevolent attitudes.

Another student summarized the drama unit in her journal.

The drama today, was for myself, the most powerful one so far. Everyone felt so strongly about what they had to say — myself included — I actually was so insulted when my family was called 'uneducated.' It felt so real, even though I'm not actually Jack Tannenbaum, and those people weren't my wife/daughter/sister — although, like the community of Kensington at the meeting, our school has provided the same kind of community, where if something like this happened, we would stick together. I felt so stupid when he had my picture taken beside his assistant because I had said that a memorial library could be useful. How could I have just done that? I expect that some people probably would have actually gone through those few feelings as the "speakers" kept on shooting us down, by telling us we had no control. It did get me thinking, though by the end, almost like they had brainwashed me. I actually thought, "Maybe a factory wouldn't be so bad, if we were helped to relocate and rebuild our businesses, and if there was a Holocaust Library to teach people of our suffering, so as not to repeat itself in the future."

We can find many different genres of writing embedded in this extended drama unit. How did the students know which format would suit their writing needs? Why is their work so intense, such a complex blend of affective and cognitive learning? In Nancy's classroom, writing is a vital and necessary part of the curriculum. For certain, Nancy's students see themselves as writers.

Building Language Power

Spelling

I consider myself an adequate speller, but there are word demons that still stump me. I have developed some skill at recognizing when a word does not look right, when I think that it may be misspelled. I was surprised when I asked ten colleagues in my faculty to assess their own spelling competence, and they to a person labeled themselves as inadequate spellers. Is it because they are now using academic references that require constant confirmation or specific terminology? Or do they, like most of us, simply need to check their spelling? On my computer, most of my errors are typos created by my inadequate keyboarding skills and, of course, my spell-check program brings up all American/Canadian spelling differences but misses homophones consistently.

Proficient spellers, then, have a high degree of competency in frequently used words, and find multiple resources for the challenges that occur in writing. Similarly, we can teach our students to use a variety of strategies when checking the questionable spelling of a word. (I am pleased to see a student circling a word in a rough draft; it's good when a young speller knows what he doesn't know.) Students need to raise their spelling consciousness.

The more exposure students have to reading and writing, to the strategies of spelling and to a variety of spelling resources, the more they will reinforce and strengthen their spelling patterns. Research has shown that spelling is developmental and increases and improves over time. Teachers need to keep the requirements of standard spelling in perspective, and assist students in learning to spell with a variety of strategies. Each new piece of information gained about how words work alters the student's existing perception of the whole system of spelling in English. Sometimes, students may appear to regress as they misspell words they previously knew, but they may be integrating new information about words into their language background.

We can organize mini-lessons and demonstrations, incorporating a wall chart or an overhead projector and calling attention to spelling problems students are experiencing (e.g., doubling final consonants, adding *-ing*). Approaches to solving a problem can be verbalized and visualized, and students can learn how an effective speller uses words. A brief conference can help a student come to grips with a troublesome word or pattern.

HELPING STUDENTS WITH SPELLING

- Students need to attend to the appearance of words and to check their encoding attempts. As students try to spell words, they often discover the underlying rules of the spelling system.
- Learning to spell is clearly related to students' general language development. Students go through developmental stages in learning to spell, but not necessarily sequentially or at the same rate.
- Spelling is not just memorization; it involves processes of discovery, categorization and generalization. Spelling is a thinking process. Students learn the patterns, regularities and unique features of spelling as they read, write, play with and attend to words. We can draw students' attention to specific patterns or groups of words to help them see a rule or generalization.
- Struggling spellers need to focus on a small amount of information at one time, especially in examining connections among words and word families. We need to help struggling spellers with particular strategies for learning and remembering words patterns—word families, mnemonic tricks, personal lists.
- Most of us fix up our misspellings as we go along, correcting those words we already know—"one minute" words—rather than wait until we have finished. We can teach our students to do these quick checks, heightening their ability to know when a word looks right.
- They can circle the word in doubt. When they return to it, they can write it over until it looks correct. They should find a pattern or generalization that applies, or say the word slowly, stretching out the sounds. Teach them to picture the word "in their mind."
- Before we tell a student how to spell a word, we need to ask, "What do you know about this word?" and build on the student's knowledge.
- Computers can help students develop a means for identifying and then correcting errors during revisions.
- Writing is the best way to learn about spelling.

✓ The dictionary and spell-check are last resorts. We want to encourage students to practice their word-solving strategies before turning to a reference. Dictionaries are valuable resources for literacy, especially for expanding vocabulary, but only if they are used as aids in authentic language events (e.g., checking the spelling of a word in a report, usage of a word in a poem). Many kinds of dictionaries can be found in a literacy-centred classroom (e.g., computer, etymological, slang, proverbs). Multiple copies of different dictionaries are useful for students looking up word information and noting differences in style, content, mode of recording and so on. Games and cooperative activities can help students to see the many uses of dictionaries in supporting their literacy learning.

✓ We can make words available and accessible to students by supplying resources of correctly spelled words around the classroom: labels and signs, class word banks, personal dictionaries in their writing folders, references (e.g., dictionaries, atlases, thesauruses), word charts of common errors, theme words, puzzles, key vocabulary from a text, content words, family words, common word patterns; they can check for the word they need in the poem they are reading about, in their personal word list, in a textbook or on a chart on the wall; theme words are not useful for teaching patterns, but may be helpful when posted around the room. Often we ask a friend nearby. We need to use all the clues we can.

✓ We can use misspellings from a first draft to help students understand patterns and their exceptions. Dealing with a few errors at a time can help them note a misspelling and develop appropriate strategies for editing.

✓ Books of jokes, riddles and puns and collections of tongue-twisters provide enjoyable reading. At the same time, they encourage auditory and visual discrimination and speech articulation.

✓ Puzzles and games can be incorporated to demonstrate a pattern or an exception. Crossword puzzles are available from many sources for a variety of levels. Computer programs allow students to make their own word lists and clues to make crossword puzzles.

✓ Board games that involve reading, spelling and cooperative skills motivate students and encourage learning. They can also be used in cooperative learning lessons to encourage working in a group.

✓ Literature provides many opportunities for word play: poems full of fascinating words used in unique ways, novels where the context supports the meaning of new and unusual words.

Handwriting

Handwriting used to be a time-consuming component of the elementary school curriculum, but in recent years teachers have realized that students need to focus on what they are trying to say, rather than just on the shape of their letters. Using a computer, we can select fonts that amaze the eye and strengthen the words. However, handwriting can help the student notice words and letters—their shape and size, their uniformity and design. Students' writing can become more sophisticated as they develop control and aesthetic awareness. Often art activities enable them to notice how cursive writing can help communication. It is important that teachers not dwell excessively on the quality of the students' handwriting, but that they encourage students to focus on cursive writing as they revise their ideas and feelings. Handwriting should be readable, uniform and aesthetically pleasing.

Style grows over time with each student, but it is important to demonstrate the formation and flow of letters with mini-lessons when necessary. Practicing handwriting should be kept to a minimum, but careful handwriting should be a part of each writing revision.

Grammar and Usage

For many years, teaching specific grammar lessons to the whole class was thought to have an impact on the students' writing. Research today tells us that students learn about language by using it and then by noticing how it is used. Learning when to use standard and nonstandard English depends on the context of the situation, requiring appropriate usage rather than correct usage. We usually speak the way our community speaks, and to alter language patterns requires creating a positive community environment and encouraging frequent interaction with significant models—speakers, coaches, peers—and, of course, listening to stories and poems, incorporating patterns in our storytelling and writing.

However, it is useful for students to examine language, detecting differences in their own oral and written language forms, as well as observing the language used by authors. Students may benefit from knowing common terms, such as *noun* and *verb*, when discussing how language works so that they can add knowledge about English to their language repertoire.

✓ The object of this game is to create a long, interesting sentence that relies only marginally on the use of "and." One student begins by giving the first word of the sentence. The next student adds a word and so on until a sentence is formed that cannot be continued. As students become familiar with this activity, add further limitations; for example, only three adjectives per noun, or only two adverbs per verb.

✓ The students can translate the following nonsense sentences into English, substituting words where necessary, or make up a grammatically correct sentence filled with nonsense words, then trade sentences with a partner who identifies the various parts of speech.

Comedic is an enurient grof with many fribs. It granks from corite, an olg that cargs like lange. Corite grinkles several other tarances, which garkers excarp by glark ing the corite and starping it in tranker clarped storbs.

116

✓ The students begin with a basic sentence: "I saw a caterpillar." They add on to the sentence—for example, "I saw a green caterpillar"—and continue until the sentence can no longer be expanded. You can have group contests to see who can create the longest sentence.

✓ Write down a sentence on a strip of paper. Cut out the words, mix them up and then ask a student to unscramble the strips to make a sentence. To take the pressure off, you may suggest to the student that she or he put the words in the order that makes the most sense, while insisting that no answer is wrong. Vary the length of the sentences according to ability and grade level.

✓ Give the students a sentence and have them rewrite it in as many ways as possible. The one criterion is that the meaning of the sentence remain unchanged.

✓ There are other interesting activities in *Literacy Techniques*, a book written collaboratively with my class of student teachers.

FOUR

Strategies for Teaching

Developing a Framework for Literacy

Think of all the diverse and language-rich resources we could find to fill our classrooms: some we can use as read aloud material; some will work well for demonstrating a particular point; some will be part of the language play that brightens our community time; some will be effective as the shared text for our small group time; some will support independent reading; some will act as models for the students' own writing, and some will be there just to strengthen our own resolve as literacy teachers.

- novels—contemporary and classic—at different reading levels, added to throughout the year
- nonfiction by authors who craft their writing
- publishers' anthologies—full of useful, short selections for working in small groups
- picture books that offer students in the middle years an aesthetic experience with words and visuals
- magazines, both to be read and to be used as art resources for responding and creating
- taped versions of books of all kinds, for struggling readers and for gifted readers
- interactive computer software and the Internet
- poetry anthologies to be read and to be listened to, that would be undiscovered unless we introduce them
- letters, memos and advertisements to use in our demonstrations
- student writing that highlights the writer's craft or that represents emotional power
- teacher writing that illustrates who we are as learners

- bits and pieces saved from the texts of our lives that we need to share with our students
- songs to read aloud as we sing the lyrics together
- book talks, discussions, guest speakers, video clips—voices from outside the walls that resonate within
- jokes, riddles, puns, funny anecdotes, riddles, tongue-twisters, rhymes—all representing the play of language
- selections from newspapers students may not find in their homes, along with articles and reviews from free community newspapers and magazines
- references such as dictionaries, thesauruses, writing handbooks, books of quotations, etc.
- computer programs, software and Internet connections

Each day, if we jot down the language resources we have used in our lives at school, we should be surprised at the amount, the quality and the variety. Those literacy experiences enrich our programs while at the same time nourishing our students.

Organizing a Literacy Program

The way we organize the classroom is important in supporting our teaching and the students' learning. A predictable schedule gives cohesion to their jumbled lives. When students are secure in the order of daily events, know where materials are located, understand the expectations and recognize how to monitor their progress, they can behave as a community of readers and writers. *Creating the Dynamic Classroom: A Handbook for Teachers* by Susan Schwartz and Mindy Pollishuke helps teachers make links between philosophy and practice.

ORGANIZING QUESTIONS

- Where and how will the students sit?
- Is there suitable access to quantities of learning resources—picture books, novels, poetry anthologies, references, nonfiction?
- How are the books organized: by reading level, by genre, by author, by series, by theme or topic?
- Where do students store their materials: books they are working on, writing notebooks, reading journals, projects?
- How do students hand in work to be read, edited or assessed by the teacher? Are there different bins or trays for separate completed tasks?
- Are there materials for the teacher to use during mini-lessons: charts, paper and markers, stick-it notes, an overhead projector?
- Where do students meet for whole class sessions, small group work, independent reading and writing?

- Are computers available for research, revision, editing and publishing?
- How are supplies for response activities and writing projects stored and made available to the students?
- How are student tracking sheets submitted and distributed?
- How will I keep track of the accomplishments of each student?

Building a Literacy Program

Each teacher will need to design a literacy timetable for the reading workshop and the writing workshop that suits the particular needs of his or her classroom. In some cases, the teacher will combine the two areas and create an integrated literacy program. The following lists of components should be seen as suggestions for developing a timetable that allows for maximum literacy growth for each of your students. In designing your program, you will need to consider all the different factors you have to deal with in your particular school setting.

TIMETABLING A LITERACY PROGRAM

- What types of activities will best suit the concepts that will be learned in the time period?
- What are the timing and resource requirements for activities in each workshop?
- How much time will be needed for preparation, completion of activities, clean up, follow up activities and discussions, reflection and evaluation?
- Will students have the opportunity to work as part of a whole class group, as part of a small group, and on their own in order to complete activities?
- Is there a good balance between activities that are mandatory and those that are free choice?
- Which aspects of the curriculum are not integrated?
- Have appropriate amounts of time and effort been allocated to activities?
- Have timing, transitions and pacing been considered from the student's perspective?
- Do activities address a range of learning styles, needs and interests?
- Will all students be challenged by the activities? Will all students be included in the teaching and activities?
- Does the program allow students to take responsibility for their learning, or is it primarily teacher driven?
- How will reflective assessment be carried out?

Meeting Time

During the community meeting time, we can accomplish a variety of activities:
- Set the agenda for the day's reading events.
- Summarize the previous day's work.
- Read aloud to the class: book talks, poems, folk tales and excerpts from novels.
- Discuss the responses you have finished reading, and read aloud responses by students that relate to issues under discussion.
- Recognize general questions that have arisen from the students.
- Demonstrate and conduct mini-lessons on concerns or needs.
- Present guest speakers or student panels.
- Conduct a special drama session.
- Involve the students in shared reading activities using overhead transparencies, charts, common texts and demonstrations.

Group Reading

Students work in a variety of groupings throughout the year:
- literature circles organized by theme, author, or genre
- engaging in response activities
- writing in reading journals
- participating in guided reading sessions

Independent Reading

Students read silently books of their own choosing:
- reading books connected to literature circles
- reading books from the classroom library
- participating in teacher conferences
- writing in reading journals

THE WRITING WORKSHOP

Meeting Time

The teacher and students meet as a community to participate in
- morning messages
- shared writing activities
- research projects
- developing rules and regulations
- creating newsletters

- teacher demonstrations
- modeling the phases of writing
- publishing completed drafts
- introducing new resources and materials
- listening to volunteers reading drafts and completed works aloud
- dividing into groups to discuss issues
- brainstorming topics and generating ideas for process writing
- engaging in mini-lessons on a variety of issues
- exploring formats and audiences for the writing
- exploring revision and editing strategies through shared proofreading sessions
- conducting ongoing assessment with the students

Independent Writing

Students participate in developing their writing projects:
- developing writing projects
- keeping personal journals
- writing letters
- conducting research projects connected to the curriculum
- participating in conferences

Guided Writing in Groups

Students work in groups:
- focusing on specific strategies
- demonstrating the craft of writing
- collaborating on a shared writing topic

Word Study

Students engage in directed activities promoting language growth:
- exploring how words work, word recognition, word games, word histories
- expanding their understanding of how sentences work
- examining how stories work
- participating in language games
- keeping a personal spelling word list

CURRICULUM-CONNECTED READING AND WRITING

Students connect their writing projects to curriculum areas:
- recording observations in science and mathematics
- keeping notebooks for social studies, health, etc.

- developing projects for individuals and groups in subject areas
- sharing projects with the class community
- writing in role in a drama unit
- publishing techniques in visual arts events

Organizing Classroom Book Collections

Linda Cameron, a colleague of mine, has been doing research with text sets. She reminds me that people have favorite authors, genres (she knows many murder mystery junkies), themes or issues (diet book devourers) and even particular formats. Whenever Linda enters a bookstore, she heads right for the children's section and hunts down the latest Cynthia Rylant books, checks out the newest releases for books on a number of topics that she collects, then passes by the sale bins for a "quick pick." The next stop is the parenting and teaching sections, followed usually by the cookbooks. This is how she shops for text sets; she reads in text sets.

A text set is a collection of any number of and types of texts that have some real connection to one another. Text can be defined as a book, an article, a poem, a movie or video, a chapter, a piece of music, a sermon, a sign—something that communicates and holds meaning. What Linda means by *connection* refers to a meaningful relationship between or among the texts: theme, topic, issue, genre, author or illustrator, story structure, historical time frame, receipt of a certain award, being a curriculum resource, raising the same question or answering a question, being different versions of the same tale or being about similar characters or from similar settings. Obviously different individuals will see different connections, and a text set will mean something unique to every reader during each reading or rereading. Time, place and experience are some of the things that alter our perspective-taking and meaning-making. Linda says,

> A second reader of the text will add a new dimension, another whole text to connect with. If a reader talks with someone about a text, that discourse is another text in which both readers will be constructing meaning. Their meanings will not be the same, and neither will their understandings of the discourse. Even that conversation is a text. If a group of people responds to a text or to a text set and they share ideas, the richness of the construction of meaning is enhanced exponentially.

TAPED BOOKS

Tapes provide an alternative way for students to experience repeated readings of favorite stories, songs, chants and poems. Their low cost and simple operation make them an ideal resource for every classroom. Many community libraries and bookstores carry a wide assortment of book tapes for people of all ages.

The auditory reinforcement of tapes, when combined with the visual image of print, is extremely successful in breaking down barriers for ESL readers and for readers who are experiencing difficulties.

The tape recorder is a powerful, nonthreatening tool for struggling middle-grade or older students. Using books read and taped, students can follow the text at their own pace to work on phrasing, fluency and comprehension. Some teachers find time to tape (or have other students tape) pages of a text for a struggling reader to build fluency and self-esteem. Students can also listen to an assigned section of the book on tape, following along in their copies.

Genre Study

By focusing on and teaching about different genres in texts, we can help students look at reading and writing experiences in different ways, increasing the breadth of literacy experiences and deepening their understanding of the function of particular texts.

Organizing units around different genres can help students in exploring, comparing, describing and assessing types of books and various forms of writing. Understanding genre may eventually help them to explore and experiment with their own writing styles and formats.

We can set up a class library of books in the genre being studied, and encourage students to select books and bring in resources of their own that they think complement the study. We can discuss with the students characteristics or rules of the genre in question, comparing these characteristics with other genres studied, and charting similarities and differences, and organize writing projects in which students are engaged in constructing their ideas within the genre.

Demonstrating Reading and Writing Strategies

When we demonstrate our own thinking out loud, we make our processing of ideas visible to our students, so that they see how we handle a piece of text before we read, while we are reading and after we read. When students have opportunities to see our own thinking processes in action, they may be able to apply similar strategies in their own work.

It is helpful to choose a text that is easily accessed, so that students can focus on their reading strategies. Select a short text that will enable you to say aloud what you are thinking as you read it through. You might begin with a passage that you have thought through first, or use a sight piece that will give the students an authentic picture of how readers read.

You can share the text on an overhead transparency or give the students a copy for them to follow.

1. Begin by revealing your own background knowledge about the content of the piece.
2. Examine the structure of the selection and draw attention to any text features or cues that may help build understanding.
3. Read the text aloud and tell the students what you are thinking as you go along.
4. Share all the connections you are making as you proceed with the reading, thoughts triggered by a specific word or an idea.
5. As you speak your thoughts aloud, draw attention to any unusual or difficult words or terms.
6. Reveal the questions that arise about your understanding of the text so that the students can see how real readers work in order to make sense of what they read.
7. Explain how you solve any difficulties that disrupt or confuse your understanding.
8. As you complete the reading, share aloud your synthesis of the meanings you have negotiated with the text.
9. You can model and demonstrate your own reading strategies using a similar think-aloud technique whenever the class needs to understand how a reader handles meaning-making with a particular type text. You can also ask students to conduct a think-aloud session once they are aware of the reading strategies that they can model.

Conducting Mini-lessons

Mini-lessons are my time for telling, demonstrating, instructing, reading aloud and sharing my accumulated wisdom about reading and writing—the big issues as well as the nuts and bolts. A mini-lesson is a brief, focused lesson that allows teachers to demonstrate or teach a specific skill or idea in a short, purposeful way. Reading, writing and thinking strategies can all be demonstrated using mini-lessons, which are often generated by the needs of the students. As well, mini-lessons can be used to review classroom procedures, to show ways to think about what one has read and to teach specific reading skills. They present a frame of reference for what the expectations will be during the reading and writing workshops.

You can select a topic for a mini-lesson based on your observation of student needs and interests, or by considering the curriculum goals. Mini-lessons can focus on a topic that is essential for students to learn, such as the routines and procedures for independent reading or how to acquire effective reading strategies. We need to be clear and explicit in our teaching and provide a summary of the lesson to remind students to use what they have learned as they engage in their own literacy work.

Conferring with Students

Conferences are essential in developing a community of readers and writers and should be a part of each school day. While there are several types of conferences, and each has its own structure and purpose, all conferences share the same general goals. Through the use of student-teacher conferences, we can encourage students to extend their exploration of a text or we can assess and evaluate their writing progress. In addition, our support during the conference helps to promote the sharing aspect of reading and writing and encourages students to feel they are members of a literacy community. The conferences should take place in a relaxed atmosphere where students feel secure and comfortable in expressing their feelings about what they have read.

How we participate in conversations with a student or with a small group of students will often determine the success of our conferences. We need to engage the students in dialogue, so that we can acquire information about them as readers and writers, and also decide on whether we should offer specific help or just be supportive of their efforts and accomplishments. We need to confer with each of our students as frequently as possible, either as a brief check-in or an in-depth conference.

We can begin the conversation by inquiring about the students' progress, the books that they are reading, or the writing being developed. Students can read aloud a section they have enjoyed from the books they are reading, or share some of the writing they are revising. We can encourage them to connect their reading and their writing to other literacy events they have participated in, or we can deal with particular difficulties they are encountering, offer suggestions, or share models that may redirect them. It is important that we encourage them to reflect on their own development as readers and writers, to guide them into becoming aware of their own successes and challenges, so that they can move towards independence as literacy learners.

Grouping Readers and Writers for Continuous Learning

The process of creating and recreating effective groups is one that evolves as we become more familiar with our students. We need to observe and assess their abilities on an ongoing basis, and note the processes and strategies they are developing. We want to gather students together in groups that are flexible, groups in which they feel comfortable sharing their thoughts and reactions while working on specific strategies.

✓ Form groups based on reading interests, activities and topics students want to explore. Consider dividing your class into four large groups on a heterogeneous basis; within each group you can select a small group of students who need specific guidance. However, for many activities, the students will belong to the larger group and not feel segregated.

✓ For students learning to read or who are having difficulty reading, we can group and regroup students for short periods where, with peers who share similar reading problems, they can focus on an applicable topic or strategy.

✓ Assess texts to determine if they meet the needs of the students who will read them. There should be a variety of texts available to each group.

✓ Allow for students' preferences in forming groups, which can include working with friends, exploring a particular genre in depth or studying the work of a specific author.

✓ Assess all students at various points throughout the year using a range of diagnostic instruments. This includes observing each student's progress in strategies for reading and writing.

✓ All members of the class should view groups as flexible. Groups should change on a regular basis and for a variety of reasons.

Sharing the Reading

All the members of the class, including the teacher, are part of the community of readers. One way to strengthen your literacy community is to gather the students together to share and support each other's work. We often read independently, but our power as literate humans is acquired from the connections we make to the responses and comments of other members of the community.

It is important to build a classroom community that encourages a cooperative and respectful atmosphere for all members. Language arts offers a context for these sessions, as we need a forum for sharing the many facets of literacy: planning, the day's schedule, discussing current issues, reading aloud significant literature, presenting interactive mini lessons on the many different aspects of reading; listening to talks by guests such as authors.

Teachers can invite students to share their thinking in pairs, in threesomes or with the whole group as they reflect on, extend and/or reinforce the application of the day's mini-lesson, evaluate how their personal reading is going, summarize what was learned or assess how their literature group is working together. The teacher can take a quick review of the status of the class as the students inform the teacher of their personal reading progress: each student can share the book title, page, any other information asked or the goals they have in mind for the rest of the day's work.

There are many ways in which community reading can take place—we, as teachers, can lead the discussion and model the use of strategies (how to question a text and how to raise discussion issues); students can read silently; the group can read the book aloud; students can read the text with a partner; or agreed-upon pages can be read together while others read silently. Whole-class guided reading sessions can offer unique chances to observe students in a large-group setting—their level of participation, their ability to follow a discussion, their ability to raise relevant issues, and their use of strategies for understanding. As well, you can demonstrate how books work.

- They can listen to you reading aloud from a variety of genres, selections they might not choose for themselves.
- They can talk about what they are reading, commenting on each other's reading and asking questions.
- They can share items from the book, reading aloud significant lines or passages.
- They can share responses they have made in their reading journals.
- They can present questions that are arising so that others may be able to offer help.
- By using stick-it notes as a tool, students can find spots in their books they would like to share.
- They can read aloud first lines or last lines or special words or phrases that have significance.
- They can read their favorite piece of dialogue aloud.
- Students can participate in sharing a poem or in choral reading.

Reading Aloud to Students

One of the most enjoyable tasks in my career has been to read aloud to students all over the world, in classrooms, libraries, auditoriums, cafeterias, wherever we can gather together. It is a time-honored activity, and watching the faces of those young people, having again and again the value and power of story affirmed, gives me courage to continue. I am always on the lookout for sources that will hold young audiences from the beginning page. The first time student teachers read aloud to a class it is a daunting, if not terrifying, experience for them, especially for the young men. But their elation when they discover the children actually listening and learning moves them on to seeking other occasions for sharing texts. We need to remember, as Pinnell and Fountas tell us, that reading aloud is instructional time, and to be aware of the choices we make and how these events can support and extend our programs. Our students should expect these reading and listening occasions as a regular part of their program. There are many opportunities throughout the day to share an excerpt from our own reading that connects to the curriculum, a selection that extends the written work a student has shared, an article from a newspaper or magazine concerning a recent issue or a picture book by an author from a different culture. When we read aloud to students, so much can happen:

- we build a community where reading is an accepted and valued practice for everyone
- we model our own respect for and satisfaction in texts
- we demonstrate how proficient readers read, the strategies we use and our fix-up techniques
- we can choose texts that differ from those our students select, opening up their worlds of literature and increasing their options for future independent reading
- we provide models of writing so that student writers can borrow and absorb the components of the writer's craft
- we let students consider and respond to the issues and ideas, the characters and conflicts in the text, freed from their print struggles so that they can focus on deep and engrossing higher level thought
- we provide real reasons for careful, engaged listening

As teachers, we can contribute to the sense of community by providing plenty of opportunities to read aloud to students, often materials they normally would not experience. Novels, for example, when read aloud a section at a time, can become a high point of the day, and a time when students can anticipate gathering together to hear the next installment. When we choose books that support a theme, we can extend students' learning; when we read newspaper and magazine articles, we can model how to find content information and how to stay abreast of current events.

This year, I was working with Gini Dickie and her grade-six students in an inner-city school in Toronto. I was struck by the quality of the community she had created with her students and the level of literacy work they were achieving together. As part of a unit on anti-bullying, I managed to provide each child with a copy of the novel *Silverwing* by Kenneth Oppel, which Gini began reading aloud to the class. It is a fast-paced adventure fantasy, full of cliff-hanging action, a perfect book to share with these students. Set in a fantasy world of a bat colony, it chronicles the perilous adventures of Shade, the runt of the Silverwing colony, who becomes separated from the others and must take a remarkable journey in order to rejoin them.

I visited the class half-way through the reading of the book, and together we explored the adventures they were listening to through improvised drama. We chose scenes from the novel, and students improvised the dialogue that would have occurred among the characters. We worked as a whole class, often in a circle, and different youngsters would participate during each scene. Because the book races along like an adventure film, there was great opportunity for developing the interactions between the characters.

Scene 1

Students volunteered to role play the female bats who had to discipline Shade for endangering their entire colony with his antics. The dialogue took place in the circle, with the student playing Shade standing in the middle. As they questioned him and tried to arrive at a just punishment, I was actually shocked at how much information they had absorbed from the teacher's reading of the text. In this scene and the ones that followed, the author's research—the bat lore and natural history—filled their talk, and strengthened the tension and drama of the moment. No one had told them to memorize the details from the novel; they were using them spontaneously to move the action along, to deepen their roles, filling the room with the wingbeats of twenty-five Silverwing bats.

Scene 2

There were five secondary students in the classroom one morning as part of their cooperative learning project. When I teach, I need everyone participating, and so the older students became the owls, enemies of the bats. They had to be persuaded to leave the bats alone, to let them migrate to Hibernaculum, their new home. In one powerful moment, the bats determined that they had to know if they could trust these owls, and one grade-six youngster asked if he could examine an owl pellet to see if the remains were bat or rat. The high-school boy as owl mimed the regurgitation of the object with such skill that the class gasped as the grade-six student took it in his hand. Of course the pellet was imaginary, but he held it in his hand, looked at it, turned and pronounced, "Rat." The work continued.

Scene 3

The stories of the bat history and culture were lost during the fire in their tree home. I asked the students to remember one of these tales and to tell it so that the wisest elders could memorize them again to continue the history of the colony. The stories they told were of births and deaths and dangers and victories and journeys. They were full of every detail one could imagine, drawn from the text, placed in the new context. And they used the names the author had used—Greek and Latin names, and the Biblical names of angels.

We improvised several other scenes, taking the incidents from the book, and reinterpreting the events with our own improvised words.

When I later returned to the class, the book had been read completely, and the students had chosen for me the name of Icarus. They lined up to present me with the stories they had previously told aloud, now written on dark purple paper with silver pens. As one by one they read to me their memory from the colony, I shook their hands and gave each a copy of the sequel novel, *Sunwing*.

Where do you want to teach? I have decided: in this classroom, in the most difficult area in my city, beside this enabling teacher and alongside these students, all of us engrossed in a fantasy world of the Silverwing bats. I would rename the school immediately—it would be called Treehaven, the first home of the colony.

A postcript: I found a Kenneth Oppel site on the Internet, along with dozens of questions for teachers to ask and demand their students answer after reading each chapter. But there was also a fine interview with the author that students would enjoy. Use manuals, even electronic ones, if you feel you need them, but be selective and professional in your choices. By the way—the secondary co-op students each asked if they could have a copy of the novel.

Reading Picture Books Aloud

At first, middle-years students may be uncomfortable with picture books. But today, we have so many fine ones that work on every level, the age of the students seems almost irrelevant. The words and images in picture books work together to synthesize a new creation, which appeals especially to today's visually oriented students. Picture books open up opportunities for discussion and therefore deepen understanding; the pictures draw the eye and the text catches the imagination. The words can offer powerful language input for students, new and unusual vocabulary, varied syntactic patterns, strong contextual clues for exploring meaning, characters who struggle with life's problems—sometimes symbolic, sometimes very real. Illustrations in picture books run the gamut of styles and techniques—watercolors, woodcuts, lithography, photography, and collage—they illuminate the text; they extend the words into possibilities of meaning; they shock the reader/listener with new interpretations, lifting the student's own experience into different conceptual realms. The old is made new; the new is made relevant. The picture book is a demanding medium, especially for older readers. I have enjoyed sharing these picture books with students of all ages:

Allen, Judy, *Tiger*
Angelou, Maya, illustrated by Jean-Michel Basquiat, *Life Doesn't Frighten Me At All*
Bradby, Maria, illustrated by Chris K. Soentpiet, *More Than Anything Else*
Browne, Anthony, *Voices in the Park*

Bunting, Eve, illustrated by David Diaz, *Smoky Nights*
Fletcher, Ralph, illustrated by Kate Kiesler, *Twilight Comes Twice*
Gaga and Friends, *Pass the Celery, Ellery*
Gerstein, Mordicai, *The Seal Mother*
Gerstein, Mordicai, *The Wild Boy*
Innocenti, Roberto, *Rose Blanche*
Martin, Rafe, illustrated by David Shannon, *The Boy Who Lived With the Seals*
Myers, Christopher, *Wings*
Polacco, Patricia, *The Keeping Quilt*
Polacco, Patricia, *Thank you, Mr. Falker*
Ringgold, Faith, *Aunt Harriet's Underground Railroad in the Sky*
Rochelle, Belinda (ed.), *Words with Wings*
Rylant, Cynthia, *The Relatives Came*
Say, Allen, *Grandfather's Journey*
Scieszka, Jon, *Squids Will Be Squids*
Smith, Charles. R, *Rimshots*
Thayer, Ernest Lawrence, illustrated by Christopher Bing, *Casey at the Bat*
Wallace, Ian, *Boy of the Deeps*
Wisniewski, David, *The Golem*
Yee, Paul, illustrated by Harvey Chan, *Ghost Train*
Yolen, Jane, illustrated by David Shannon, *Encounter*

Shared Reading

Years ago, my English consultant Bill Moore would come into my classroom with a number of poems he had prepared and, before he read, he would distribute copies of them to the students. I can still recall the absolute joy I felt with this ritual: my grade-eight students would hear powerful words by authors they hadn't met yet, read aloud in a marvelous voice as they followed along with their own copies. Afterwards, Bill would involve them in choral speaking or poetry writing, and when he left we still had his poems to return to later and our own writings to share. No one ever thought that he was teaching; we just knew that we were learning. And he always had complete attention from those kids. What greater gifts could there be for a new teacher?

Today, reading aloud to students while they read the same text silently seems a contradiction in teaching outcomes. How can they gain reading strength if they are not meeting reading challenges on their own? The answers lie in our reasons for engaging in shared-reading activities with the class at a particular time with a particular text. We don't want students staring mindlessly at a text selection while the teacher drones on, nor do we want students to read aloud without reason or preparation, one after the other. Shared reading needs to be an engaging and interactive process in which our students notice the sounds and shapes of words all at once. When I read a poem aloud, I want them to see the words as their ears hear them; I want the students to notice how the oral text and the written text mesh. Often I will read from an overhead transparency, from a computer text and graphics presentation, from the textbook they are using or from distributed paper copies. Once in a while, I read aloud a novel, or the first chapter of one, while they follow along, especially with readers who are having difficulty. (Taped books and CDs with song lyrics are other interesting examples.) I use this technique for guided practice sessions as well, where I can focus on an issue and highlight my own thinking process as I think/talk aloud. Of course, this method is a staple of our writing programs, where we often share our own work and student writings in demonstrations or celebrations. I am hoping that the learning that happens will be transferred to their independent reading and writing activities. I will never forget the child who felt he could not read the novel he had chosen, and when I said that I would read every other chapter to him as he followed along if he read the ones in between, he smiled and agreed. That is just what I did, and he told me that it was the first novel he had ever read.

I know that reading is a complex process that requires modeling, and when I share a prepared reading that lifts the words from the pages in front of their eyes, the students make connections that might not have happened otherwise. I can use the experience as a source for all kinds of literacy learning.

Shared-reading occasions with students in the middle years is a strange hybrid of strategies, but it has amazing results when used as part of a complete literacy program. I know, because Bill Moore showed me.

Guided Reading Instruction

Guided reading works as a teaching strategy because it lets us observe students as they read, while they are in the process of reading, rather than after they have completed their attempts at making meaning with the text. Instead of struggling to stop them from racing through to complete the questions they know are waiting, we can help them notice the strategies they are already incorporating into their reading, introduce new ones that may be useful in supporting their challenges and help them connect their lives to the text. After they read along silently in a small group for a while, we can help them stop and notice the strategies they are using and the ones they might try in order to make informed decisions as they construct meaning. We can model the questions effective readers ask while reading, helping students to become aware of how fluent, proficient readers "think with text." We want to guide young people toward becoming independent and successful readers.

Guided reading involves grouping students who have similar reading abilities or who need to acquire similar strategies for reading success. Unlike traditional reading groups, where membership is static, guided reading groups reform constantly throughout the year. The goal of these programs is to have all students read increasingly sophisticated texts—both fiction and nonfiction—and develop strategies they can use independently. A supportive atmosphere is crucial to guided reading, as is ongoing observation and assessment. Guided reading activities should develop into literature circles and book talk sessions as soon as the children are reading with some measure of independence.

Books used for guided reading can be grouped according to level of difficulty. The most important consideration in assigning a level to a book rests on whether students at the level can read at a rate of 90–95 percent accuracy. For each level, there should be several books. Our groups will contain a range of readers and the books we choose for them must reflect this reality. Guided reading collections can take time to build and, to begin, you will likely need the help of colleagues, including the school librarian, to find copies of the same book. Selections from school anthologies represent another useful source of reading material.

A crucial component of any guided reading session is the time devoted to discussion of the text—identifying connections the students made, discussing interesting vocabulary they met in the reading, assessing the accuracy of their predictions, identifying ways in which the text relates to their life and sharing reactions and insights. We can direct students' attention to points in the text that support their knowledge (e.g., sound-letter relationships) or we can ask them to apply particular strategies. Together, we can revisit parts of the text or do a second reading of text to help students increase fluency. Students can then discuss the strategies they used while reading, those they need to develop further.

In a guided reading program, we can assess our program by the students' development and whether they are becoming successful independent readers. We can ask ourselves these questions: Are the students flourishing in their reading program? Are they becoming readers who participate willingly in the act of reading? Do they happily anticipate reading sessions? Do they choose to read independently?

Literature Groups and Book Clubs

In our schedule for literacy growth, we need to create time for students to work in groups with shared copies of books they have self-selected from a limited selection we have provided. As their ability to follow the routine of participating in literature groups progresses, students may make suggestions of books to be added to the resource. They may decide to choose to read different books by the same author, or books on a connected theme.

Heterogeneous groups are formed on the basis of students' book choices, and this creates a structure for conducting literature circles with the class. Each group should meet two or three times a week in order to carry on a continuing conversation about their books. They will need to decide on how much should be read before each session—what I call "checkpoints"—and, if they read ahead, group members should reread the portion that will be discussed. The in-depth discussions can be supported by the notes, comments and sketches they have prepared in their reading journals while reading the text.

During the literacy conversation, participants can include their own personal insights, their emotional responses, connections they are making to the text and to the comments of others. As they begin to hitch-hike on each other's comments, they are building background knowledge and incorporating new meanings and different perspectives into their own world picture. It is important that they speak up and take turns, and refer to the text when making a point. They should be sure that each member participates and supports each other's comments, moving the discussion along and helping to keep the talk focused on the ideas generated by the text. Through these conversations, they learn to support their ideas with references in the texts, to pose questions that have real significance and to accept, or at least consider, the opinions of others when they disagree. They will be involved in thinking and reading about the text in a collaborative activity as they interact with others, learning about themselves as they deepen and expand their meaning making.

As teachers, we need to establish the routines that will make possible the management of literature groups in the classroom, making the expectations clear and repairing any disruptions in the flow of the work through demonstrations and direct instruction. We can contribute to the functioning of literature circles in a variety of ways, depending upon the needs of the group or individual students. Sometimes I am a silent participant, observing and gathering information concerning their reading behaviors, their group dynamics or their comprehension strategies. At other times, I model and demonstrate effective ways to contribute to a discussion. I can act as a facilitator, making positive comments that support and affirm the contributions of the students, encouraging them to refer to the text to provide evidence for their ideas and moving them toward analyzing and synthesizing their thoughts as they move along in the conversation. And there are times when I need to intervene directly about problems they are having with the text, pointing out information they have missed or clarifying a complex issue. I can restate a point for emphasis, synthesize the ideas they have presented or extend the direction of their thinking on an issue. But my teaching/learning goal has to be to guide the group's growing ability to monitor their own progress, so that they can take charge of their learning and move themselves into a deeper and more meaningful discussion. They will be building their storehouse of knowledge about literature and authors, of how texts work, learning from inside their own constructions.

✓ Throughout the year, I use my reading-aloud time for students to respond by talking together as a community and in small groups. This helps them understand how to think and talk about the literature we have heard or read. I carefully select the text—often a picture book with many-layered meanings; I also like short stories and poems for these events, and find selections in classroom reader anthologies useful. I read the selection with as much ability as I can muster, organize the response activities and conduct a feedback session on the completion of the reading and the responding. I structure the response questions the first time, or at least set a context for the discussion, and use the experience as a demonstration of how we work with literature. Sometimes I have each group discuss a different aspect of the text, creating a real reason for sharing afterwards. Since students used to ask to see my copy after they had listened to it, in order to confirm or argue different points, I started to make copies of the text available to them. Working with one group in a fishbowl demonstration can help students see how text conversations work, and what roles should be filled if we are to all benefit from this structure. After the experience, I like to analyze the process with the students so that they can break down the process into manageable units that will offer us a means for discussing their own progress later on.

✓ A few moments for guided reflection, oral or written, at the conclusion of each session will help the students assess their own contributions and the quality of the group's participation. They can share comments, questions and insights, and make decisions about the direction the next meeting should take, such as clarifying their roles to strengthen the subsequent discussions.

✓ Sometimes at the conclusion of a literature discussion of a book that has had an impact on them, students may want to become involved in a response project, individually or cooperatively, where they explore an issue or theme in the text. At times, I will suggest an activity to them that suits the book or that supports a need the students have revealed.

✓ What book groups can the students find out about, and which ones can we share with them? They could observe Oprah Winfrey when she presents one of her book-club shows, listen to the participants in conversation with the author, report the titles of her choices of books to read. Teachers on staff may belong to a book club; the public library may have a similar group. Students may have parents or friends who gather together to talk about books they have read.

✓ Sound recording a group's book talk can offer a powerful demonstration of the kinds of text talk the students are engaged in. As well, sections of the dialogue—critical moments in the discussion—can be transcribed by either the teacher or a group of students and used as a text for group members to observe their own thinking in progress. Accompanied by an analysis of the strategies that are being demonstrated, this report could be part of their self-assessment review two or three times a year, a record of their own reading progress.

GUIDELINES FOR TAKING PART IN A READING WORKSHOP

Preparing for the reading workshop

Select books that you think you'll enjoy and abandon books that aren't working for you after you've given them a good chance.
Read the book twice.
During your second reading take notes. This will affect your contribution to the conversation. The better the notes, the better the conversation.
Always have the book with you so you can refer back to it for support.
Focus on questions that do not have a right or wrong answer and can be useful for discussion.
Say what you believe, even if the rest of the group disagrees.
Give everyone a chance to talk, and listen to what each person has to say about the topic.
Piggyback on ideas to develop them further.
Help group members understand words or situations they don't understand.
No put-downs. Respect other people.

Role of facilitator

Checks to see that team members are prepared
Helps keep the conversation going
Gives points for others to add to, when needed

Encourages everyone to speak
Stays with open-ended questions
Treats everyone with respect
Makes statements (not questions) to guide the conversation, such as

"Let's discuss why...."
"Tell us what you mean by...."
"Tell us why you agree...."
"Let's talk about...."
"So you're saying...."
"I'm wondering...."
"Explain what you mean."
"Let's look in the book."
"Tell us about that."

Role of group member

Reads the book carefully and prepares notes
During the discussion, refers to notes and to the book
Expresses how and why they feel the way they do
Stays with the topic/question
Adds on to a speaker's comments
Asks questions for clarification
Uses polite language
Participates in the conversation with comments such as

"I think...."
"I agree...."
"I disagree...."
"I'd like to add...."
"I'm confused about...."

Reading Independently

During independent reading, students select books and read them silently, but the difference between this strategy and that of individualized reading is that, while both increase the time students spend reading in school and provide opportunities for learning and practicing reading strategies, independent reading offers explicit instruction and encourages students to monitor their own reading. The teacher's role is to guide the selection of the books and to increase reading competence through book talks, conferences and mini-lessons, and promoting reading journals. Your role as a teacher is also to model reading during reading time by reading your own books as well as offering productive instruction. I like to promote independent reading during the community time with a book talk featuring new additions to the classroom library, new books by favorite authors, books that I need to "sell" to the students because they are less familiar, books on relevant issues or connected to the media or books representing different genres. You can talk about the issues involved in the story, connect the book to other books and issues, give a brief outline of the book, talk a bit about the plot or the people, show the cover or illustrations and offer a personal response, being careful not to overinflate your influence as the teacher.

Students should be encouraged to read at their own pace, using books they've chosen to read. We can ensure that they can make good choices by including a range of books in our class and in the school library, and by giving advice and help if asked. We need to represent a wide genre of books, including nonfiction, novels, folklore, poetry and picture books. While a few should be classics, most should be contemporary. Over time the students' concentration can be extended, as can the level and range of reading material. Often, because we need to build an atmosphere in the classroom, we begin our program at the beginning of the school year with uninterrupted and sustained silent reading time, and then gradually introduce an independent reading program. By keeping up-to-date records of the books they have read, students can notice their reading patterns and widen the range if necessary.

The Ten-Novel Project

During the first term of school, Larry Swartz introduced an individualized reading program in his classroom: students would choose books independently and read during a daily silent reading time. He noticed, however, that many students in the class were choosing a different book every few days. Also, the students were choosing picture books or poetry anthologies which they could finish in a twenty-minute reading session. He had some concerns that they were not deepening and extending their reading, and decided to move these students into reading novels. As well, he wanted to introduce a system where the students reflected on their reading and shared their thoughts about books with others in the classroom community.

When the class came back from the holiday break, he invited the students to participate in The Ten-Novel Project. Students were given a week to find ten novels from the classroom collection, school or community libraries or their own books. These were to be the books they hoped to complete by the end of the school year. Each student was given a small cardboard box to decorate and use to store their novels. If students chose to abandon a novel, they were required to replace the title with another—this often happened when friends told each other about books they read or when new orders came in from the book club.

Each student was given a folder to decorate with a title page featuring a slogan or quotation about reading, which they found on posters or books in the classroom. On the next page, the students listed the ten novels they hoped to complete, and this list served as a contract for their future reading. The following two pages featured a reading inventory to be completed by each student. They were given a number of pink tracking sheets to record their daily reading—date, title of book, number of pages. For each novel they completed, they were required to complete a bright yellow response sheet, which they could share with their friends, bring to a reading conference or store in their folders. Occasionally, Larry would introduce a whole-class response activity (e.g., a character's journal entry, a character web, a vocabulary treasure hunt) that would also be kept in the folder. This process gave the students guidance and support, making them see that this activity mattered. They came to realize that independent reading was to be an important part of their program.

The Writing Workshop

In a writing community, each member's work is considered significant, and feedback and dialogue are needed and valued. Rather than having students view their writing as an assignment to be finished as quickly as possible, the writing workshop, when used as a regular classroom routine, can help them recognize the significance of generating meaningful topics and the need to revise and edit as they move toward final drafts. Students become more proficient by writing at regularly scheduled times for authentic purposes—real reasons for behaving as writers. They come to know their own developing abilities, what needs to be worked on and what can be celebrated.

An important component of a successful writing program is the inclusion and maintenance of predictable, regular writing times. Teachers need to familiarize students with elements of the writing process and the inherent time commitment for each stage—drafting, revising, rethinking, redrafting, editing and publishing. Setting up classroom routines that everyone understands is the foundation of the writing workshop. Students are secure in knowing what is expected; they can request a conference if they are having difficulty; they know there is a time frame that allows for drafting and revision in class, and they recognize their own worth as members of a writing community. Because students are writing every day, we can develop their understanding of the conventions of writing through mini-lessons, and they actually practice these points within their composing events.

1. You can begin the writing workshop with a brief talk about writing, using examples from picture books, novel excerpts, biographies of writers, or your own life's writing. Teachers need to share their own stories with students and encourage students to author their life histories as readers and writers. As well, teachers need to use their own writing as a model, sharing copies of notes and memos, demonstrating a writing event (such as creating a parent newsletter), showing that writing remains a significant aspect of adult life. Students need to see teachers revising, struggling, crossing out, adding and moving text, referencing and publishing.

2. This can be followed by a mini-lesson related to the aspects of writing you want the students to understand, or those drawn from your observations of student needs. You need to focus on some aspect of writing that the students can then apply to their own writing. Students can take notes in their writing journals for future reference. For example, students can participate in an interactive editing session with an example of work you copy onto a transparency. The students can alter the text in a variety of ways—combining sentences, choosing alternate words, spelling, noticing attributes of words.

3. Students usually write independently for half an hour or more while you confer with individuals or small groups to offer guidance and feedback. During independent writing, students are engaged at different times in a variety of activities, but they will either be writing or working on some aspect of the writing process—focusing on a topic in their notebook, working in a small-group peer sharing, revising their structure, using resources and references, editing for accurate use of conventions, preparing for publication or conferring with the teacher. Students can choose a project they would like to work on, and can decide if they want to work alone, with a partner or as part of a small group. Students should write silently and move around only when necessary. Conferences can be conducted in quiet conversational tones.

Here are some examples of projects students could be working on:

- composing an anecdote drawn from their personal experience
- writing and illustrating a story to be read to younger classes
- writing a play
- publishing a magazine or a class newspaper
- rewriting a speech
- preparing and conducting an interview

- writing a poem
- completing a research project

We need to engage the students in their writing so that they will want to continue the writing process, which means re-thinking and revisiting their writing to develop strength or clarity, to alter its organization or to select effective words and language structure.

There should be a variety of writing materials: special notepads, clipboards, graph paper, poster board, stationery, pens, markers, pencils and computers—what students write on and with can have surprising effects on the quality of their work. For example, different types of stationery for correspondence can alter a student's approach to the task.

Students should be aware of the purpose and audience for their writing assignment. This awareness will help them to generate ideas, as we write for a variety of reasons:

- to entertain (stories, poems, skits, plays)
- to inform (reports, labels, tests, invitations)
- to direct/teach/learn (dialogue, directions, notes)
- to persuade (speeches, ads, editorials, stories)
- to express personal feelings (journals, poetry, stories)

They need to consider authentic audiences for their writing:

- self (diary, journal)
- friends (notes, e-mail)
- classmates (reviews, recollections)
- parents (letters, invitations)
- teachers (reports, dialogue journals)
- known and unknown audiences (computer networks)

The international educator Gordon Wells has taught me so much about the functions of writing in our lives. In his book, *Dialogic Inquiry*, he offers four basic requirements for our programs if we are to have any effect on the writing development of our students, and these directions work at the heart all of our efforts:

- The writing projects the students are engaged in must have significance for the other members of their community.
  (We want to participate in these literacy events. Our classroom community recognizes that we need to write as a life process.)
- The topic needs to be of interest to the writer, who must believe that there is more to discover about it.
  (I want to write about this topic; it continues to interest me. There is something more out there in the world to discover than what I know right now.)

144

- The writer needs to care enough about the aesthetic quality of the writing so that he/she will attempt to solve problems that arise in the process of creating it.

  (I want to revise my work for you; it matters. I want you the reader to have access to my thoughts, my information and my feelings, and to notice how I have ordered and arranged them.)
- The writer must be able to count on members of the community to provide support and resources when he/she feels it to be necessary.

  (I want you to help me grow as a writer when I ask you, and I will support you in your efforts as well.)

Students can consider carefully what they want to say, how they will say it most effectively, the writing craft that will strengthen its effect and the proofreading that will facilitate communication. Then you, as chief editor, can review the final draft before it is published, shared publicly or placed in the student's folder. Labeling and numbering the first and second drafts can help students keep track of each version of each writing project. Having writing folders for each student can facilitate classroom management; these folders can be kept in boxes or crates. In the folder students can also keep a sheet recording their writing projects, the type of writing and the date completed.

Students need be familiar with a variety of references and resources, including dictionaries, thesauruses, charts explaining how specific conventions work and, of course, computer strategies such as spell-checks.

Nancy Steele runs in-depth reading and writing workshops. Having read many of her students' writings in this book, you will have seen her success in promoting and supporting writers. Her philosophy of teaching is evident in her exciting program:

> The first thing I try to do is change the ideas that the kids have about writing. When they come to me, most of them think they can't write and if they do think they can write, what they enjoy writing seems to me to be generally meandering and pointless fantasy. My first job, then, is to convince them that they have stories to tell and that they can tell them so that other people will be interested in reading them.
>
> We talk first about what might make a good story. They need to be convinced that being chased by a shark or struck by lightning might not necessarily make a more interesting story than redecorating your room or going for a peaceful morning dip at the cottage. Luckily, I have a huge collection of great writing by kids their age about all the normal things that happen to everyone. I read these to them. I also make sure these collections are always out during reading time for students who have left their novels at home.

First term is story writing. Grade 7 stories must be based on reality. Grade 8 students may write fiction if they insist but I make it clear that I am very demanding about fiction. Historical fiction must be accurately researched. Sci-fi must actually have a point in reality. They are much better fiction writers after "true story" training. Many of the grade 8 students stay with stories from their lives.

I think it is important that the writing conferences are safe places. Only positive comments are allowed until the author has agreed that s/he wants advice. By the end of grade seven the students in the writing classes make all the suggestions I would have made about each story. They are less adept at helping each other with poetry, but they often collaborate with each other on plays. I try to get as many poets, playwrights, novelists in to talk to the kids as I can. They teach me so much.

I also try to teach note-taking, webbing, research skills, paragraphs, essay form, response journal writing, summarizing etc., but these all happen in my other subject areas. I think it is important that writing units have their own time slot in the year. Perhaps you could integrate them thematically, but you might lose the attention to the detail necessary for each.

The Writing Conference

The goal of any writing conference is to support the students' writing development. We need to act as wise and compassionate instructors and editors do with adults. I have worked with hundreds of graduate students, mainly teachers, and they have represented as complete a range of abilities as any grade in any school. Most need help in choosing and focusing on a topic; most need help in finding resources to support their projects; most need help in revising their ideas, rearranging sections, moving chapters, adding and clarifying details, finding references to support their opinions and validating final drafts. A doctoral thesis will not be accepted until it is bound in leatherette with embossed title on the cover. In other words, everything matters.

In my own writing, including the writing of this book, I have depended upon friends and colleagues to listen to my initial plans and to give me feedback on my first drafts, to listen to my concerns about choosing the most appropriate voice to convey my messages, to add to my book lists, to share and describe literacy events in their classrooms. How, then, are we to work alongside students encouraging, instructing and guiding their writing development? How should we proceed?

Pinnell and Fountas suggest that students co-direct the conference, "analyzing and evaluating their own writing projects and initiating questions about their own writing" (p. 56). A conference may last one or two minutes, or be a longer engaged conversation. You can hold a writing conference at any time during the writing process—at the beginning of an idea to be developed or during the revision of a draft. It is an opportunity to help students clarify what they want to write about, to offer feedback about what they have written and to reinforce what they are learning as writers.

PROMPTS TO USE IN WRITING CONFERENCES

What are you working on?
Do you want help with your writing?
I'm interested in this idea. Tell me more.
Why did you want to write about this topic?
Have you changed your mind while working on this topic?
What do you see in your mind's eye?
What do you want the reader to remember about your piece?
What is the most important point you are trying to make?
Do you think you have more than one topic here?
What is your favorite part?
Could you cut a piece out and use it in another project?
What about looking back at your idea web, or making a new one?
Do you need to find more information?
Where did this event happen?
What happened to cause this event?
Would a reader understand this part?
Can you expand this description?
Can you add your own reactions and feelings?
Why does this part matter?
Do you think a reader will care about this character?
Will a reader hear your own voice?
Read your lead aloud. Will it work for a reader?
How to you want the reader to feel at the end of the piece?
I am having trouble understanding this part. Can you help me to clarify it?
Have you thought of trying another pattern?
What about chunking the lines in your poem differently?
Do you think any illustrations might help?
Read this quotation aloud to me. Does it sound like real people talking?
Would adding some dialogue help in this section?

Larry Swartz collects books in which fictional characters write down their lives, and he shares them with his students throughout the year as motivation and inspiration for their own lives as writers. For example, *Catherine Called Birdy* by Karen Cushman (1994) is a fictionalized diary set in medieval times that tells about young Catherine's attempt to find an appealing suitor. *Out of the Dust* by Karen Hesse (1997) is told as a series of poems by fifteen-year-old Billy Jo, who relates the hardships of living on her family's wheat farm in Oklahoma during the years of the depression. *Feeling Sorry for Celia* by Jaclyn Moriarty (2000) is a novel filled with letters written by Elizabeth's mother, and describes a young girl's humorous adventures growing up in Australia. In *Monster* by Walter Dean Myers (1999), sixteen-year-old Steve Harmon is on trial as an accomplice to a murder and tries to come to terms with the direction his life has taken; the book records his experiences in prison and in the courtroom in the form of a film script and journal. We can find so many different novels today written in different formats, useful demonstrations of the very strategies you are trying to share with your students.

Building Word Power

I used to call classroom time for word study "Word Power." We can include a word study session each day during our literacy meetings, sometimes presenting just one point we want to bring to the attention of the whole class. Mini-lessons focusing on common patterns in groups of words or meaningful generalizations can also be held two or three times a week. Students can record their notes in a word study book or in their writing journals, along with their personal word lists. We want to promote information and discovery about language with this interactive structure.

In the spelling time each week, students focus on learning to spell particular words and patterns chosen from their writing, or words they need help with. These should be significant words they will need to learn to use. Students can focus on about five words during each session.

You can revise the types and use of spelling tests so that students can learn from the experience. They can choose the words they want to be tested on; older students can volunteer to assist in testing difficult words; students can discuss their problems in finding strategies for coping with misspelled words.

Mini-lessons for Word Power

✓ Students can play with words:
— change a verb to a noun (walk–walker)
— change the tense or person of a verb (call–called, she calls–I call)

— change an adjective to a noun (tired –tiredness)
— change the number, case, and gender of nouns (boy–boys, boy–boy's, actor–actress)
— change the degree of adjectives (costly–costlier–costliest)

✓ We can discuss with the students how new words are added to our language.
— acronyms (scuba = self-contained underwater breathing apparatus)
— abbreviations (ad = advertisement)
— portmanteau words: words created by blending two words together (smoke and fog = smog)
— words that came from names (sandwich is named after the fourth Earl of Sandwich, who liked to eat his food between two slices of bread so that he could continue to gamble)

✓ Mnemonic devices are word associations that we use to help us spell difficult words, homonyms, and so on. (The principal is our *pal.*) Students can make their own mnemonic devices.

✓ Students can make lists of words, classifying them by
— letter clusters (ae, oo, ou, ight, tch)
— compound words (rainstorm, snowball)
— portmanteau words
— suffixes and prefixes
— number of letters
— number of syllables
— homographs: words that are spelled the same, but sound different
— homophones: words that sound the same, but differ in meaning
— silent letters, rhyming words, plurals (ways of forming), contractions (can't, shouldn't)
— abbreviations (i.e., e.g., etc.)
— word families
— anagrams rearranged to make other words (wasp/paws)
— palindromes (level, did, madam)

✓ They can explore the patterns that occur in English.
— Vowel sounds/combinations
— Letter combinations (gh, dge, qu, tch)
— Suffixes (glamour/glamorous, labor/laborious, grief/grievous)
— IE or EI: *i* before *e* except after *c*
— Double Letters (occur/occurring but offer/offering)
— Forming Plurals (s, es, ies, ves)
  – irregular plurals (e.g., mouse/mice, sheep/sheep, larva/larvae)
— Silent Letters (b in climb, k in knife, l in walk)

— Prefixes (well+fare = welfare, but well+ made =well-made)
— Endings (able/ible, ence/ance, ise/ize)
— Soft and Hard *C* and *G* (crack/centre, gentle/get)
  – courageous, peaceable, gracious, staging
— Odds and Ends:
  – homophones: there/their/they're, past/passed, no/know

Supporting Special Needs Students

> They were teaching us rats to read. The symbols under the picture were the letters R-A-T. But the idea did not become clear to me, nor to any of us, for quite a long time. Because, of course, we didn't know what reading was. Oh, we learned to recognize the shapes easily enough, and when I saw the rat picture I knew straight away what symbols would appear beneath it. But as to what all this was for, none of us had any inkling.
>
> *Mrs. Frisby and the Rats of Nimh*

Margaret was a student in my first year of teaching grade five, and she could read aloud fluently and with expression. She enjoyed acting as a helpful monitor with classroom routines, and I appreciated her support. However, while preparing for the parent interview, I read her Office Record Card, which indicated that she was a below-average student working to the limit of her potential. When I approached the principal about the discrepancy between the official assessment and my own observations, he suggested that I interview her about what she had read, and that I was in for a surprise. I followed his advice as a new teacher should, and found out that she had no understanding of what she had read, and could make no sense of the text. I had, for months, missed who she was as a reader, basing my judgment on one simple literacy process: her oral reading during a group read-around time. I was totally unprepared and unable to offer her appropriate instruction, but my compassionate principal explained that some students are automatic decoders and nonreaders at the same time. His words directed me into a lifetime of attempting to understand this strange and complicated process called reading.

Students who are struggling with their reading and writing have diverse needs and abilities, and Margaret is but one example. For teachers, this makes working with them complex indeed. One published set of texts, or a series of remedial exercises, just can't support alone the different approaches we will need to use as teachers in designing programs for these students. Inappropriate instruction may delay or regress a student's growth.

✓ Students in difficulty need to experience what successful literacy events feel like, to know that there is hope for recovery, that they will be supported in their struggle to grow toward independence.

✓ When students arrive at school in the morning, they will see that in our literacy classrooms, everyone and everything matters.

✓ We may need to help these students set short-term goals or to break the complete task into smaller steps. They will need brief but regular conferences and checkpoints, in order for us to offer support and to provide direction that will move them ahead toward success.

✓ All readers need our time and attention, but troubled readers in particular benefit from individual attention.

✓ During sharing times they, too, need to present to the class, and can do so with extra preparation and support. They need to show the books they have published, to present a book talk about a book they have read and enjoyed, to read a poem they have practiced, or to share excerpts from their journals.

✓ Most of all, students in literacy difficulty need to be recognized for their successes in the processes of reading and writing, to have their accomplishments celebrated.

✓ We need to help these students struggling with reading to learn the problem-solving strategies that proficient readers use to make sense of print experiences. Margaret Phinney says, "They remember the meaningful, the outstanding and the useful first, and those are all determined by personal interest and purpose."

✓ We can prepare them for testing situations with demonstrations and mini-lessons. We can often orally direct them to respond to test-like questions, where the pressure to be correct is less than in a testing situation. These little practice sessions can help prepare them for the formal testing events. After a test, it is useful to stress what the student knew and understood, to build on positive aspects of the experience, and to then move into remedial work.

Assessment and Evaluation

Assessment involves the ongoing observation of students and includes, among other things, portfolio conferences, anecdotal records, formal and informal tests and self-assessment. The outcomes of our assessment procedures allow us to plan programs that reflect students' current learning and that capitalize on their strengths to develop other areas of growth. Evaluation is made up of the judgments (marks and grades) we make on the basis of our assessment practices. Assessment informs our daily teaching, and evaluation is used when communicating with parents and other educators. Since the quality of our evaluation reflects our assessment procedures, we need to assess all areas of a student's development. In order to do this we need to gather information, not only from the methods outlined here, but also from others in the school and from parents. Your assessment tools, combined with those completed by the students, can provide a well-rounded analysis of each student's abilities.

Observation

We can observe a student read for a period of five minutes, note the book, the strategies used, aspects of the text that appear to be challenging and what the student does when difficulties are encountered. Or we can watch the student for a similar amount of time as she or he selects a book, noting the amount of time the student can read independently and the amount of movement the student exhibits during the activity. We bring to the process of observing our students our knowledge of the theory of language learning and the practical aspects of teaching the students how to read.

It is important to remember that observation guides and checklists are only indicators of a student's progress. They are most helpful when they are repeated several times throughout the year so that trends and progress over the year can be noted. Their value is in the information they can contribute to the overall analysis of a student's growth. Observations arising from the checklists can then be shared with the students, in order to help them focus on areas that require change.

Portfolio Conferences

Portfolio conferences are an important source of information about the reading experiences of students. Students bring to the conference several journal entries that fuel discussion as to their growth as readers. Discussion questions may relate to the number of books read, the number of books begun but not finished and the reasons for not finishing books. Based on the results of the conference, you can conduct reading inventories and/or set new goals—e.g., setting a number of pages, books to be read, books from another genre—and work together to assess reading progress. As well, your conferences with students are essential for the development of their self-assessment skills.

Portfolio conferences can take place between you and the student, between peers or between the student and the parent. Of these configurations, teacher-student conferences are essential, peer conferences are desirable and student-parent conferences are recommended. Only when you have had a conference with each student should the students participate in peer conferences. Ongoing teacher-student conferences may also culminate in student-led parent conferences at the end of the year.

KEEPING A PORTFOLIO

Does your portfolio reflect who you are and what is important to you?

Is your portfolio a showcase of your growth?

Does your portfolio reflect your ability as a student?

Is your portfolio a good balance of all your subjects?

Does your portfolio allow you to look back on your learning?

Does your portfolio reflect your strengths and the areas that need growth?

Does your portfolio reflect what you've learned, what you are working on and what you want to learn?

Do you share what is in your portfolio with your parents?

Do you share what is in your portfolio with other students?

Do you allow your teachers to help you decide what should be in your portfolio?

Are you proud of what is in your portfolio?

Anecdotal Records

Anecdotal records are those we make on an informal basis as we observe students in their day-to-day learning. This can be done either on an individual basis or with groups. Given the nature of these observations, many teachers choose to make dated notes on index cards, in small notepads or on stick-it notes. At the end of each week these notes can be transferred to letter-sized paper and stored in the student's folder.

Anecdotal records may also take the form of inventories, where students complete a list of their achievements, favorite activities and interests. These can be extremely helpful when planning topics to explore in class. Inventories can also tell you about a student's feelings related to aspects of their learning, information that may not be visible in class. Students can complete inventories with their parents when they begin the school year, and in-class inventories can be created and updated throughout the year.

Formal and Informal Tests

Formal and informal tests are helpful when they assess learning that is measurable and when they reflect the content of the program. You and the students should view test results as a way to check the effectiveness of the program. If, however, information gleaned from tests does not reflect your ongoing assessment, the testing device may need to be amended or—in a less likely scenario—your ongoing assessment may need to be altered. Keep in mind that if both the test and the instruction are sound, there are still a number of reasons a student may not perform well on an isolated test. These range from a bad night's rest to a problem at home. These factors must be taken into account when discussing test results. We also need to consider the fact that one test for all may not be the most effective measure.

Self-Assessment for All of Us

Knowing that self-assessment will form a part of their overall assessment helps students develop a sense of ownership of their learning and know that they can shape the course of their learning. Their contributions in conferences, journals, portfolios and discussions are all part of the self-assessment process. Sharing in their assessment helps students to recognize what they know, what they need to know and ways in which they can learn. Students begin to see themselves as readers and writers, thinkers and meaning makers.

In addition to assessing and evaluating students, we also need to evaluate our teaching programs so that we can check on the program's ability to meet the goals we set for students. In part, program evaluation arises from the progress students make. We need to ensure that what we do in class, from selecting texts through assessing a student's responses, are sound and valid, and contribute to our students' overall development.

All of us—students and teachers—need to consider our effectiveness, our progress, our sense of personal and professional satisfaction. We grow from considering our lives, reflecting on our changes, talking to others about our shared concerns, connecting other aspects of our lives to what is going on in our work and our learning. We can become what we dream we can become. I need my network of significant others to nudge and motivate and support me, so that I will look up to discover the lake on the horizon and the satisfaction of my own growth.

SELF-ASSESSMENT GUIDES

READING SURVEY

Beginning of Year

Why do people read? List as many reasons as you can think of.

How did you learn to read?

Do you like to read?

How would you describe yourself as a reader?

In general, how do you feel about reading?

What kinds of books do you like to read?

How do you decide which books you'll read?

How do you decide what you will read about?

Who are your favorite authors? List as many as you would like.

Do you like to read some stories more than once?

How often do you read at home?

How often do you read when you are not at school?

What is the best thing you have ever read? Why did you like it?

What kinds of topics do you especially like to read about?

What do you like to read—comic books, magazines, books?

Do you think you are a good reader?

Do you like long or short stories?

Do you have a favorite book?

What is your favorite book? Why?

Do you have a favorite author?

When do you read?

Where do you read?

What makes reading hard for you?

What would make reading easier?

What kinds of words do you find difficult to read?

What do you do when you can't read a word?

When you are reading and come to something you don't understand, what do you do?

Do you look at the pictures in the books while you are reading?

What would you like to do better as a reader?

Do you ever buy books? What kind?

Do you read magazines? What kind?

Do you borrow books from the public library?

Do you borrow or trade books with your friends?

Do you have a book collection at home?

Do you play games where you have to read, like Monopoly?

Do you discuss what you read with anyone?

What do you like to do in your spare time?

How much television do you watch each day?

What do you watch on television?

With whom do you watch television?

What do you want to be when you grow up? What will you need to read to do that job?

List the goals for reading that you would like to meet by the end of the year.

What kinds of stories bother you the most?

Do you use a computer?

Do you play games on the computer?

Do you like to read aloud to other people?

Do you know what kinds of books your friends like?

Suppose you had a pen pal in the same grade in a different school and you wanted to find out about him or her as a reader; what questions would you ask?

Does anyone read at home? What do they read?

Did your parents read to you when you were young?

What usually happens during reading time at school?

What would you tell a friend to do if he or she couldn't read a word?

What kind of reading group are you in? Would you like to be in a different reading group?

Do you think textbooks are hard to read?

What does someone have to do in order to be a good reader?

Who are your heroes?

End of Year

Did you find some reading material harder than others? Can you give some examples? What makes one book harder than another?

Did you discuss books with other kids?

What kind of stories bothered you the most?

How have you grown as a reader since the start of the year?

What are your favorite genres to read?

Which were the best books you read this year? What made these books good?

Who were your two favorite authors and why do you like them?

What was your favorite poem? Why did you like it?

What did you learn this year as a reader that you are proud of?

Describe the best conversation you had in a discussion group.

List the books you have read this year, and the genre of each.

A COLLECTION OF PROMPTS FOR RESPONDING TO TEXTS

Narrative Texts

What is the author's message?

What is the story really about?

Do you think the title is appropriate for the story?

Why do you think the author wrote this story?

Are different points of view presented?

What are some of the most important ideas?

Were there parts of the book you didn't understand? What puzzled you?

What questions do you still have?

What does this text make you want to learn more about?

Who was the voice the author chose as narrator—first person, third person, a storyteller, an anonymous voice, a different voice or the author himself or herself? Did this style work well?

What was more important, the plot or the characters?

Are the family relationships presented in a stereotypic way?

Where and when does the story take place?

Where else could the story take place?

Could the setting be a real place that exists in our time?

How much time passes in the story?

In another time and place, how would the story change?

How did the author control the passing of time?

Does the setting change over the person's life?

What was the mood or atmosphere of the story, or did it change as you read the book?

What music would you tell a friend to play if they were preparing to read the book?

Are there any powerful characters in the story? What makes them that way?

Who is the most important character?

Who is the most interesting character?

Which character taught you the most?

How does the author/illustrator reveal the character? (Look at what the character does, thinks, or says; or what others say about the character.)

Which characters change and which didn't? How is character change important in the story?

Who is a character that plays a small role? Why is this character necessary in the story?

What did you learn from one character in the story?

How did characters feel about one another?

What changes do the characters encounter and how do they deal with them?

What choices did the characters have?

How do a character's actions affect other people in the story?

Would the story have been different if a particular character had been omitted?

Which character did you dislike? Were you ever frustrated by one of the characters? Which character would you like to become?

How did the author help us to know what the characters were thinking?

Were there any characters who were not described at length but who could have been important in the story?

Did the characters remind you of other personalities in television or films?

Did you know enough about the characters from reading the book to believe in them as if they actually existed? Would you like to know any of them?

How are minority roles depicted?

Are there stereotypes or tokenism?

How did the author begin the story to engage the reader?

What is the story problem? How did you think it would be solved?

What was the most important part of the story?

If you were the author, would you have ended it in any different way?

What clues did the author give to allow the reader to predict the ending?

What lessons does this story teach about life?

Do you think the story really could have happened?

How does the author help you feel that you are really there (in both realistic stories and fantasy)?

What two or three sentences summarize the whole story?

Make a sketch or picture of an event in the book.

Does the story unfold over a long period of time, or is it told over a matter of days?

Did you find out about events in the order in which they would actually have happened?

Were there any plot shifts in time, space—flash forwards or flashbacks, or two stories being told at the same time?

What events in the story were not actually written, but you understood from between the lines what was happening?

Were there twists and turns in the story that surprised you?

Did you wonder what might happen next? Were there any clues about what was going to happen? Was it too easy to predict the events of the plot?

Were you able to see the events of the story through the eyes of the characters?

What would you have done if you were inside the book and you could have helped one of the characters?

Are any of the female characters strong and independent?

Whose story could you say the book is really telling?

Could the story be told if sex roles were reversed?

What are some interesting words, phrases or sentences?

Are there words that were used to create a feeling or picture in your mind?

Was any of the language especially interesting, vivid or surprising?

Was the dialogue realistic? Could you hear people in life saying those words?

Did the author use description well? Was there enough or too much?

What did you notice about the style of the writing? How did the book begin—with a question, dialogue, a shocking statement, one word? How did each chapter begin?

Were there long sentences? Short choppy ones?

Was there a common trick or convention the author used throughout the book? Did you notice any in-jokes?

Were there examples of slang, different spellings or strange words or expressions that the author used for a reason?

Did you hope an event in the book would not happen, but it happened anyway?

Did anything happen to you just as it happened in the story?

When were you first held hostage by the story and knew that you had to finish it, no matter what?

Was the author able to involve you emotionally in the story? Did you laugh or cry?

Did you ever feel that you were actually in the story being told, or did you feel as if you were a spectator or an eavesdropper?

Which character in the book did you connect with? Do you know why?

Do any of the characters remind you of someone in your life?

How is this story like any other story you know?

How are the characters, setting and problems like those in other stories you have read?

What do you know about the period of history in which this person lived?

Does this person's life remind you of other biographies you have read or of fiction texts?

How is this person's problems like the problems of people in other biographies or fiction books you have read?

What special images do you remember from the story?

Has the book become a movie? Would the story work well on film?

Was the book the right length—too short or too long? How were the chapters organized—long or short? Was the book divided into sections?

What about this book did you especially like? What do you wish there were more of in the story?

Did you choose to read this author because of the type of story she or he writes, or because of the content of the story?

Did you have any difficulties with the book? How did you handle them?

Have you read this book before? Was the second reading different?

Did you read the book in one sitting or a chapter at a time?

If you had written the book, how would you have changed it?

Did this book make you think about your own life in a different way?

Has this book influenced what you think? What you believe in? Your view of the world?

Have you learned anything about yourself or others from reading this book?

What passages from the book do you especially remember?

What quotations would you choose from this book to make a poster for your bedroom wall?

Would you recommend this book to a younger reader?

What is your favorite illustration? Why did you choose it?

Could you picture what was happening when there were no illustrations?

Information Texts

How is information organized (by topic, in time, by contrasting ideas, etc.)?

Does the total format of the text help you understand the topic better?

What does the title tell you about this text?

What genre does the selection represent? How did you know?

Is the text a good example of this genre?

How is this book like other books you've read in this genre?

What do you find difficult about reading books in this genre?

How do headings and subheadings help you find information in this text?

Are there "loaded" words that have insulting overtones?

What did you learn about this topic?

How does the story make you feel?

Have you ever had similar experiences?

Were you reminded of anything in your own life?

What does this book make you think or wonder about?

What do you already know about this topic?

What surprised you?

What have you experienced in your life that helps you understand this topic?

How does the information in this text fit with what you already know?

How does this (book, article, topic) remind you of other texts you have read?

Does this text provide useful information for you personally?

Why did the author think this subject was important?

What experiences or life circumstances led you to read about this topic?

What did you learn about life from the book, about different places, about history, science, religion, etc.?

If you were the author, would you change the order of any of the events?

What information is provided through illustrations (drawings, diagrams, maps, charts, etc.)?

Are the illustrations clear and understandable? Are they easy to interpret?

Are the illustrations explained by labels, legends and captions when needed?

Would you read other books by this author?

Have you read other books by this illustrator? How is this text similar to or different from others the artist has illustrated?

What other books does this book make you want to read?

Was the design of the cover or the book jacket effective? Did it catch your attention? Was the blurb on the back useful?

Do you know other writings by this author? A series? A sequel? An autobiography? A picture book? Have you read any of them? Can you find patterns in the things the author writes about, in the events of the stories, in the characters, in the ideas the author seems to believe in, in the style of the writing?

Have you read any information about the author, or seen a videotape of the author speaking?

Has the author used his or her own life in creating the story?

What type of research went into writing this book?

Have you read comments about the author's works, such as reviews or opinions from classmates? Do you know what the author is working on now?

Are there books similar to those of this author that you have read?

What questions would you ask the author about the book or about his or her life?

What is the author's perspective or stance toward the topic?

What has the author said that makes you question the accuracy of the information?

SELF-ASSESSMENT: READING WORKSHOP

	Yes	No	Sometimes

I was prepared for today's reading.
I made contributions to the group's discussion.
I listened to my group members.
I asked questions about the book.
I shared my opinion about the book.
I referred to the book to support my point of view.
I helped the group solve problems.
I was able to retell parts of the story.
I commented on the author's style and use of language.
I developed a better understanding of the book
because of the literature circle.

My strengths in the literature circle included

_____

_____

Areas I still need to work on include

_____

_____

My most valuable contribution to the group today was

_____

_____

Our discussion helped me understand this book in these ways:

_____

_____

These topics were still not clear to me after we finished our discussion:

_____

_____

Today's discussion would have been more helpful if we

_____

_____

WRITING SURVEY

Beginning of year

How would you describe yourself as a writer?

What do you enjoy writing about?

Do you write letters to people? Does anyone write to you?

Do you keep a journal?

Do you prefer to use a pencil, pen or computer? Why?

What would you like to learn so that you can become a better writer?

What is the best part of writing?

When you write, do you worry about making spelling errors?

What do you do when you are not sure how to write a word?

Do you ever use a dictionary? Do you ever use a thesaurus?

How much do you write about each book you read in your journal? What was your favorite journal response? Why?

Why do people write? List as many reasons as you can think of.

What does someone have to do or know in order to write well?

How do you decide what you'll write about? Where do your ideas come from?

What kinds of responses from others help you most as a writer?

How often do you write at home? In general, how do you feel about what you write?

What are your favorite genres to write?

What can you do well as a writer?

What areas do you want to improve as a writer?

What rules and conventions of writing can you use very well?

Why do you write?

How often do you write when you are not in school? Why?

How do you feel about the writing that you do at school or at home?

What is the best thing you have ever written? Why do you like it?

What kinds of topics do you especially like to write about?

What would you like to learn how to do better as a writer?

End of year

How many writing projects did you publish this year?

What different kinds of writing you did you complete? (Genres: realistic stories, memoirs, biographies, autobiographies, reports, articles, letters, etc.)

What were your favorite genres to write?

What writing projects were the best you have written? What made them good?

What have you accomplished this year that you are proud of as a writer?

What did you learn to do as a speller this year? What new knowledge of spelling do you use when you write or edit your writing?

How do you plan on improving as a writer next year?

AN EDITING CHECKLIST

Is your title engaging and representative of your project?

Reread and look carefully at the overall theme or impression you want to give the reader.

Should you add something—interesting vocabulary, an intriguing beginning or a stronger ending?

Should you take something out—things that don't make sense, confusing words, boring words, words that are repeated?

Should you move things around—rearrange paragraphs, words or sentences to make more sense, be clearer or sound better?

Did you plan for your writing (researching, note taking, brainstorming, jotting down ideas, listing)?

Are your ideas organized and easy to understand?

Do your details strengthen your topic?

Did you use examples to help the reader understand?

Is your language and choice of words understood by your audience?

Is your writing clear, concise and to the point?

Are sentences grammatically correct and do they make sense?

Are words spelled correctly?

Is the punctuation appropriate?

Are words properly capitalized?

If handwritten, is the writing neat and legible? If not, are the font and design appropriate?

Are paragraphs properly formatted?

Are quotations properly identified and formatted?

Are headings and subheadings properly formatted?

Are footnotes and/or endnotes properly identified and formatted?

Is the bibliography properly formatted?

Did you include all references?

Would it help to illustrate your work with charts or diagrams?

Would pictures or illustrations assist the reader?

Do you have a special cover for your project?

Have you submitted all the drafts?

Is your writing folder complete?

STUDENTS' GUIDE TO WRITING TESTS

Multiple Choice Questions

1. Read the question and all answers carefully.
   - pay attention to key words in the question and the details in each possible answer

2. Select your answer carefully.
   - cross out answers you know are incorrect and focus on the ones that are left

3. Use what you know in the answers.
   - focus on what you know about the topic to choose your answer

4. Do not always choose your first answer.
   - always check your response

5. Be careful of answers that contain words like "always" or "never."
   - absolute answers are rarely correct

6. Realize "best" answer may not fit exactly.
   - it is simply the most appropriate in the selection of answers

7. When you don't feel comfortable with any of the answers, make a guess.
   - you have a chance of getting it right

8. Time yourself carefully.
   - don't waste too much time on one question—you can always go back to it

Short-Answer and Extended Response Questions

1. Be sure you understand the question.
   - highlight or underline key words or phrases

2. Reflect on key words and/or phrases you want to use in your answer.
   - in the margin or on a blank page record these keywords and/or phrases

3. Organize your notes.
   - number your notes in a logical order so that they can be an outline of important ideas for your answer

4. Organize your thoughts.
   - be sure your ideas are complete, logical and detailed

5. Write your response.
   - use your margin notes as your guide

6. Reread the question and your answer.
   - be sure your answer is clear, concise and complete

BIBLIOGRAPHY

Adoff, Arnold. *The Basket Counts*. New York: Simon and Schuster, 2000.

Alexander, Lloyd. *The King's Fountain*. New York: Dutton, 1989.

Allen, Janet. *Words, Words, Words*. Portland, Maine: Stenhouse, 1999.

_____. *Yellow Brick Roads*. Portland, Maine: Stenhouse, 2000.

Allen, Judy. *Tiger*. Cambridge, Mass.: Candlewick Press, 1992.

Anderson, Carl. *How's It Going?* Portsmouth, NH: Heinemann, 2000.

Angelou, Maya, illustrated by Jean-Michel Basquiat. *Life Doesn't Frighten Me At All*. New York: Stewart, Tabori & Chang, 1993.

Applegate, Mauree. *When the Teacher Says, "Write a Poem."* New York: Harper and Row, 1965.

Atwell, Nancie. *In the Middle*. Portsmouth, NH: Heinemann, 1998.

Avi. *Nothing but the Truth*. New York: Avon Flare, 1993.

Ballard, Robert and Rick Archbold. *Ghost Liners. Exploring the World's Greatest Lost Ships*. Markham, ON: Scholastic, 1998.

Barrs, Myra and Valerie Cork. *The Reader in the Writer*. London, UK: Centre for Language in Primary Education, 2001.

Bomer, Randy. *Time for Meaning*. Portsmouth, NH: Heinemann, 1995.

Booth, David. *Guiding the Reading Process*. Markham, ON: Pembroke, 1999.

_____. *Literacy Techniques*. Markham, ON: Pembroke, 1996.

Booth, David and Robert Barton. *Story Works*. Markham, ON: Pembroke, 2000.

Booth, David and Jonothan Neelands. *Writing In Role*. Hamilton, ON: Caliburn Enterprises, Inc., 1998.

Bradby, Maria, illustrated by Chris K. Soentpiet. *More Than Anything Else*. New York: Orchard Books, 1995.

Browne, Anthony. *Voices in the Park*. London, UK: DK, 1998.

Bunting, Eve, illustrated by David Diaz. *Smoky Night*, San Diego, CA: Harcourt Brace, 1994.

Calkins, Lucy and Shelley Harwayne. *Living Between the Lines*. Portsmouth, NH: Heinemann, 1990.

Calkins, Lucy. *The Art of Reading and Teaching*. New York: Longman, 2001.

Canfield, Jack (ed.). *Chicken Soup for the Kid's Soul*. Deerfield Beach, FLA: Health Communications, 1998.

Chambers, Aidan. *Tell Me*. Portland, Maine: Stenhouse, 1996.

Cleary, Beverly. *Dear Mr. Henshaw*. New York: Dell, 1983.

Cleary, Beverly. *A Girl from Yamhill*. New York: Avon Books, 1988.

Cole, Joanna. *Inside A Hurricane (The Magic School Bus Series)*. New York: Scholastic, 1994.

Cousineau, Phil. *The Art of Pilgrimage*. Berkeley, CA: Conari, 1999.

Cunningham, Patricia et al. *Reading and Writing in Elementary Classrooms*. New York: Longman, 1995.

Cunningham, Patricia and Richard Allington. *Classrooms That Work*. New York: Longman, 1999.

Dahl, Roald. *Boy: Tales of Childhood*. New York: Puffin Books, 1984.

Daniels, Harvey. *Literature Circles*. Portland, Maine: Stenhouse, 1994.

Dawber, Diane. *My Cake's on Fire*. Ottawa, ON: Borealis, 2001.

Derewianka, Beverly. *Exploring How Text Works*. Australia: Primary English Teaching Association, 1990.

Dispenza, Joseph. *The Way of the Traveler*. Sante Fe, NM: John Muir, 1999.

Ehrlich, Amy (ed.). *When I Was Your Age*. Cambridge, Mass.: Candlewick Press, volume 1, 1996; volume 2, 1999.

Fleischman, Sid. *The Abracadabra Kid: A Writer's Life*. New York: Greenwillow Books, 1996.

Fletcher, Ralph. *What a Writer Needs*. Portsmouth, NH: Heinemann, 1992.

Fletcher, Ralph, illustrated by Kate Kiesler. *Twilight Comes Twice*. New York: Clarion Books, 1997.

Fountas, Irene and Gay Su Pinnell. *Guiding Readers and Writers Grades 3–6*. Portsmouth, NH: Heinemann, 2001.

Freeman, Yvonne and David Freeman. *ESL/EFL Teaching*. Portsmouth, NH: Heinemann, 1998.

Freire, Paulo and Donald Macedo. *Literacy: Reading the Word and the World*. South Hadley, Mass.: Bergin and Garrey, 1987.

Gerstein, Mordicai. *The Seal Mother*. New York: Dial Books, 1986.

_____. *The Wild Boy*. New York: Farrar, Straus and Giroux, 1998.

Granfield, Linda. *In Flanders Fields: The Story of the Poem by John McCrae*. Toronto, ON: Stoddart, 1996.

Graves, Donald. *A Fresh Look at Writing*. Portsmouth, NH: Heinemann, 1994.

Greenfield, Eloise and Lessie Jones Little. *Childtimes*. New York: HarperTrophy, 1979.

Hanson, Jane. *When Writers Read*. Portsmouth, NH: Heinemann, 1987.

Harris, Theodore and Richard Hodges. *The Literacy Dictionary*. Newark, Delaware: International Reading Association, 1995.

Harrison, Phyllis (ed.). *The Home Students: Their Personal Stories*. Winnipeg, Manitoba: Watson and Dwyer Publishing, Ltd. 1979, pp. 210-211, as quoted in Ian Hundey and Michael Magarrey, *Canadian History 1900-2000*, Irwin Publishing, 2000, p. 123.

Harvey, Stephanie. *Nonfiction Matters*. Portland, Maine: Stenhouse, 1998.

Harvey, Stephanie and Anne Goudvis. *Strategies that Work*. Portland, Maine: Stenhouse, 2000.

Harwayne, Shelley. *Going Public*. Portsmouth, NH: Heinemann, 1999.

_____. *Lifetime Guarantees*. Portsmouth, NH: Heinemann, 2000.

Hawcock, David, illustrated by Ian Dicks. *Unwrap the Mummy*. London, UK: Tango Books, 1995.

Heard, Georgia. *Writing Toward Home*. Portsmouth, NH: Heinemann, 1995.

Innocenti, Roberto. *Rose Blanche*. Mankato, Minn.: Creative Education, 1995.

Jobe, Ron and Mary Dayton-Sakari. *Reluctant Readers*. Toronto, ON: Pembroke, 1999.

King, Stephen. *On Writing: A Memoir of the Craft*. New York: Scribner, 2000.

Lamott, Anne. *Bird by Bird*. New York: Anchor Books, 1995.

Leigh, Nila K. *Learning to Swim in Swaziland: A child's-eye view of a southern African country*. New York: Scholastic, 1997.

Little, Jean. *Little by Little*. Markham, ON: Puffin Books, 1987.

Lowry, Lois. *Looking Back*. Boston: Houghton Mifflin, 1998.

Manguel, Alberto. *A History of Reading*. Toronto, ON: Knopf Canada, 1996.

_____. *Pictures*. Toronto, ON: Knopf Canada, 2000.

Marks Krpan, Cathy. *The Write Math*. Parsippany, NJ: Dale Seymour, 2001.

Martin, Rafe, illustrated by David Shannon. *The Boy Who Lived With the Seals*. New York: Putnam's, 1993.

Martin, Russell. *Out Of Silence*. New York: Henry Holt, 1994.

Mearns, Hughes. *Creative Power*. New York: Dover, 1929.

Moffett, James and Betty Wagner. *Student-Centered Language Arts and Reading, K–13*. Boston: Houghton Mifflin, 1976.

Morrison, Lillian. *Slam Dunk*. New York: Hyperion, 1995.

Myers, Christopher. *Wings*. New York: Scholastic Press, 2000.

Myers, Walter Dean. *Bad Boy: a memoir*. New York: HarperCollins, 2001.

Nichol, Barbara. *Beethoven Lives Upstairs*. Toronto, ON: Lester, 1993.

O'Reilly, Mary Rose. *Radical Presence*. Portland, Maine: Heinemann, 1999.

Oppel, Kenneth. *Silverwing*. Toronto, ON: HarperCollins, 1997.

Palmer, Parker. *Let Your Life Speak: Listening for the Voice of Vocation*, San Francisco: Jossey-Bass, 2000.

Parkes, Brenda. *Read It Again!* Portland, NH: Stenhouse, 2000.

Paulsen, Gary. *My Life in Dog Years*. New York: Delacorte Press, 1998.

_____. *Guts: The True Stories Behind Hatchet and the Brian Books*. New York: Delacorte Press, 2001.

Peck, Robert Newton. *A Day No Pigs Would Die*. Peter Smith, 1999.

Pennac, Daniel. *Better Than Life*. Markham, ON: Pembroke, 1994.

Phinney, Margaret. *Reading with the Troubled Reader*. Toronto, ON: Scholastic, 1988.

Polacco, Patricia. *The Keeping Quilt*. New York: Simon & Schuster, 1988.

_____. *Thank you, Mr. Falker*. New York: Philomel Books, 1998.

Portalupi, JoAnn and Ralph Fletcher. *Nonfiction Craft Lessons*. Portland, Maine: Stenhouse, 2001.

Pullman, Philip. *The Amber Spyglass*. Alfred A. Knopf, 2000.

Reynolds, David West. *Star Wars: The Visual Dictionary*. Toronto, ON: Stoddart, 1998.

Rhodes, Lynn and Curt Dudley-Marling. *Readers and Writers with a Difference*. Portsmouth, NH: Heinemann, 1996.

Ringgold, Faith. *Aunt Harriet's Underground Railroad in the Sky*. New York: Crown, 1992.

Rochelle, Belinda (ed.). *Words with Wings*. New York: HarperCollins, 2001.

Rosenblatt, Louise. *The Reader, the Text, the Poem*. Portsmouth, NH: Heinemann, 1978.

Routman, Regie. *Conversations*. Portsmouth, NH: Heinemann, 2000.

Rylant, Cynthia. *The Relatives Came*. New York: Bradbury Press, 1985.

Sachs, Oliver. *The Man Who Mistook His Wife for a Hat*. New York: HarperCollins, 1990.

Say, Allen. *Grandfather's Journey*. Boston: Houghton Mifflin, 1993.

Schwartz, Linda and Kathlene Willing. *Computer Activities*. Toronto, ON: Pembroke, 2001.

Schwartz, Susan and Mindy Pollishuke. *Creating the Dynamic Classroom*. Toronto, ON: Irwin Publishing, 2001.

Schwartz, Susan and Maxine Bone. *Retelling, Relating, Reflecting*. Toronto, ON: Irwin, 1995.

Scieszka, Jon. *Squids Will Be Squids*. New York: Viking, 1998.

Short, Kathy and Kathryn Pierce. *Talking About Books*. Portsmouth, NH: Heinemann, 1998.

Simon, Seymour. *Sharks*. New York: HarperCollins, 1995.

Smith Jr., Charles R. *Rimshots*. New York: Dutton Children's Books, 1999.

Snowball, Diane and Faye Bolton. *Spelling K-8*. Portland, Maine: Stenhouse, 1999.

Spinelli, Jerry. *Knots in My Yo-yo String*. New York: Knopf, 1998.

Stanley, Diane. *Leonardo da Vinci*. New York: Morrow Junior Books, 1996.

Stone, Richard. *The Healing Art of Storytelling*. New York: Hyperion, 1996.

Szymusiak, Karen and Franki Sibberson. *Beyond Leveled Books*. Portland, Maine: Stenhouse, 2001.

Thayer, Ernest Lawrence, illustrated by Christopher Bing. *Casey at the Bat: a ballad of the republic sung in the year 1888*. Brooklyn, NY: Handprint Books, 2000.

The Guinness Book of World Records. Enfield, UK: Guinness, 2001.

Tomlinson, Carl. *Children's Books from other Countries.* Lanham, MD: The Scarecrow Press, 1998.

Tovani, Cris. *I Read It, But I Don't Get It.* Portland, Maine: Stenhouse, 2000.

Wagner, Jane. *Building Moral Communities through Educational Drama.* Stamford, Connecticut: Ablex, 1999.

Wallace, Ian. *Boy of the Deeps.* Toronto, ON: Groundwood, 1999.

Wells, Gordon and Gen Chang-Wells. *Constructing Knowledge Together.* Portsmouth, NH: Heinemann, 1992.

Wells, Gordon. *Dialogic Inquiry.* Cambridge, Mass.: Cambridge University Press, 1999.

Wick, Walter. *A Drop of Water.* New York: Scholastic, 1997.

Wisniewski, David. *The Golem.* New York: Clarion Books, 1996.

Yee, Paul. *Tales from Gold Mountain.* Toronto, ON: Groundwood, 1989.

Yee, Paul, illustrated by Harvey Chan. *Ghost Train.* Vancouver, B.C.: Douglas & McIntyre, 1996.

Yolen, Jane, illustrated by David Shannon. *Encounter.* San Diego, CA: Harcourt Brace, 1992.

Yolen, Jane. *Here There Be Unicorns.* San Diego, CA: Harcourt Brace, 1994.

INDEX

ACKNOWLEDGMENTS

Kids Can Press for "After English Class" by Jean Little in *Hey World, Here I Am!*
Harcourt Brace for "The Promise" by Jane Yolen in *Here There Be Unicorns.*